P R A C T I C A L   G A R D E N I N G

ROSES

PRACTICAL GARDENING

ROSES

DAVID SQUIRE

Published in the USA in 1995 by

J G P R E S S

Distributed by

W O R L D P U B L I C A T I O N S , I N C .

The JG Press imprint is a trademark of JG Press, Inc.

455 Somerset Avenue, North Dighton, MA 02764

Designed and produced by

T H E B R I D G E W A T E R B O O K C O M P A N Y

Art Director and Designer Terry Jeavons

Managing Editor Anna Clarkson

Series Editor Penny David

Illustrator Vana Haggerty

Studio photography Guy Ryecart *assisted by Jim Clowes*

Location photography Steve Wooster *assisted by Carolyn Clegg*

Typesetting and page make up Mark Woodhams

ISBN 1-57215-028-9

Produced by Mandarin Offset

Printed and bound in China

CONTENTS

INTRODUCTION

Roses are remarkable shrubs, native only to the northern hemisphere but enjoying a world-wide popularity that no other plants can equal. The shapes of their flowers range from Species roses with fewer than eight petals to many-petalled Hybrid Teas (now known as Large-flowered roses) and Floribundas (now known as Cluster-flowered roses) with forty or more petals. Their colours are just as varied. Some have a single colour, others are a fusion of shades which often change as a bud opens. The shapes and habits of the roses also vary from ground-hugging forms to those that can be planted in hanging baskets or are such vigorous climbers they can cloak tall trees in colour. Their attractive qualities are not limited to the shapes and colours of their flowers – scent, is perhaps, their most magical quality. The scent of roses ranges from a delicate sweetness to rich fragrances with hints of fruits and spices. Hips, also known as heps, are the seed pods of roses and in autumn the colours of some deepen into rich shades, introducing an additional element to growing roses.

There are roses for all situations, whether in garden rose beds, planted in tubs, window boxes and hanging baskets, displayed on patios or scaling walls and climbing into trees. They are also excellent for forming flowering hedges, and some have the bonus of colourful heps in autumn. Many roses are also excellent for cutting and displaying indoors or for presentation – just one romantic red rose or a beautiful bouquet.

FLOWER COLOURS

Terms used to describe the colours of flowers include:
- Single colour: One colour.
- Bi-colour: The colours on the inside and outside of each petal are different.
- Blend: Two or more colours on each petal.
- Multi-coloured: Colours markedly change with age.
- Hand-painted: Centre is light-coloured and delicately feathered merging with other colours towards the outside.
- Striped: Two or more colours in bands or stripes.

Flower types

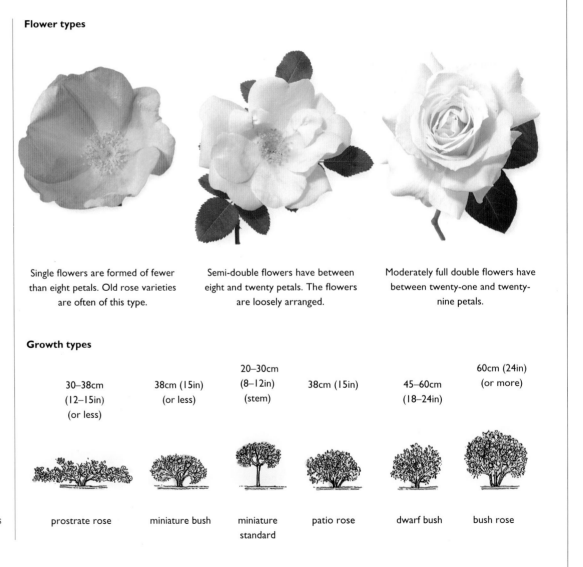

Single flowers are formed of fewer than eight petals. Old rose varieties are often of this type.

Semi-double flowers have between eight and twenty petals. The flowers are loosely arranged.

Moderately full double flowers have between twenty-one and twenty-nine petals.

Growth types

prostrate rose	miniature bush	miniature standard	patio rose	dwarf bush	bush rose
30–38cm (12–15in) (or less)	38cm (15in) (or less)	20–30cm (8–12in) (stem)	38cm (15in)	45–60cm (18–24in)	60cm (24in) (or more)

FLOWERING TIMES

Roses flower over a surprisingly long period during summer, some just once, others repeatedly.

• Single flush: Also known as 'once flowering', refers to roses which generally have only one flowering period, usually in the latter part of early summer and into mid-summer and lasting for several weeks. Occasionally a few flowers appear later, but not sufficient to create a spectacular display. However, there are some Ramblers and Shrub roses which flower in late spring, early summer or late summer.

• Repeat-flowering: Also known as 'recurrent' and 'remontant', these roses have two or more flushes of flowers a year. Where a variety produces flowers between the main flushes, these are known as 'perpetual' and 'continuous' flowering, but these terms can create a false impression about the flowering period, which is neither perpetual nor continuous.

The creation of varieties which develop flowers throughout summer has been the aim of many rose-breeders. Recent years have seen the introduction of English roses (see page 107) which combine a wide colour range and the recurrent flowering nature of Old roses.

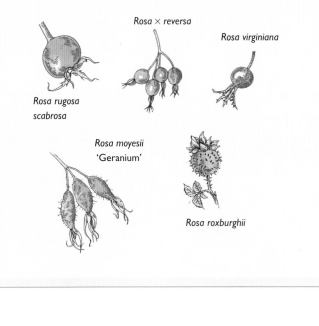

FRUITS

In autumn, many shrub roses develop fruits known as hips or heps. These are varied in size and shape, some are round and large, others flask-like, while a few are prickly. Roses with attractive hips include:

Rosa macrophylla 'Master Hugh' (very large/red); *R. moyesii* (flask-like/red); *R. moyesii* 'Geranium' (flask-like/red); *R. moyesii* 'Sealing Wax' (flask-like/scarlet); *R. pimpinellifolia* (small/black); *R. roxburghii* (prickly/red); *R. rubrifolia* (brown-red); *R. rugosa* 'Alba' (round/red); *R. rugosa* 'Fru Dagmar Hastrup' (bright red); *R. rugosa* 'Rubra' (round/red); *R. rugosa scabrosa* (large/red); *R. soulieana* (oval/orange-red); *R. virginiana* (small/red).

Rosa × reversa

Rosa virginiana

Rosa rugosa scabrosa

Rosa moyesii 'Geranium'

Rosa roxburghii

Full forms of double flowers have between thirty and thirty-nine petals.

Very full forms of double flowers have forty or more petals.

75cm (2½ft) (stem)
half-standard

1m (39in) (stem)
full-standard

1.3m (51in) (stem)
weeping standard

2.1–2.4m (7–8ft)
pillar rose

1.2–1.8m (4–6ft)
miniature climber

2.1–9m (7–30ft) (or more)
climber

2.1–9m (7–30ft) (or more)
rambler

THE RANGE OF ROSES

The earliest roses were wild roses and include many still popular in gardens, such as the Damask rose (*Rosa damascena*), the Provins or French rose (*R. gallica*) and the Scotch or Burnet rose (*R. pimpinellifolia*, but earlier and often still known as *R. spinosissima*). Others were natural crosses between species and include *R. × alba*, the white rose of York which is thought to be a hybrid of *R. gallica* and the dog rose (*R. canina*). Roses from Asia spread into Europe gradually over the centuries, but it was not until Chinese roses were introduced between 1792 and 1824 that the cavalcade of new colours and the repeat-flowering varieties appeared. Roses such as Noisettes, Bourbons and Hybrid Perpetuals were created then and the introduction of the first Hybrid Tea in France in 1867 brought the most dramatic changes. This rose was called 'La France' and brought further variety and vitality to rose growing. Floribundas were introduced in about 1934, from crosses with Hybrid Teas.

ABOVE The Gallica rose 'Duc de Guiche' reveals large, double, intense crimson-magenta flowers which open flat and are usually quartered. It is a relatively new Gallica rose, introduced in 1829, and forms a shrub about 1.2m (4ft) high and wide.

BUSH ROSES

Hybrid Tea and Floribunda roses are the most widely grown types and are extensively featured in this book (pages 28 to 65). They are arranged according to their colours, with pages 48 and 49 detailing Hybrid Teas which are famed for their scent, and pages 64 and 65 detailing scented Floribundas. They bring an exciting dimension to gardens.

RIGHT 'Constance Spry' is a New English type of rose bred in England by David Austin Roses. It bears magnificent clear-pink blooms with an old-fashioned appearance.

ABOVE The Rugosa type 'Pink Grootendorst' was introduced in 1923, originating as a sport from 'F. J. Grootendorst'. Rugosa roses form dense shrubs with luxuriant foliage and grow well even under poor conditions.

RIGHT The Modern Shrub rose 'Fritz Nobis' was introduced in 1940. It forms a shrub about 1.8m (6ft) high and wide and creates a mass of clove-scented, fresh, clear-pink flowers with a few yellow stamens. In autumn it develops a feast of magnificent dull-reddish heps (fruits) which last well into winter. It creates a superb display even on light, sandy, poor soil.

LEFT The Floribunda 'Playboy' creates a mass of orange-yellow flowers shaded scarlet. Floribunda roses are now properly known as Cluster-flowered roses.

The Hybrid Tea 'Cordon Bleu' develops moderately scented, pinkish-apricot flowers. Hybrid Tea roses are now correctly known as Large-flowered roses.

CHOOSING A ROSE

When selecting the type of rose to grow it is all too easy to consider just Hybrid Tea and Floribunda varieties. There are many others and some, such as Shrub roses, are ideal for adding to shrub borders, where they introduce an entirely different character, distinctive fragrances and delicate colours. Many of these are featured on pages 98 to 107. Their names are frequently steeped in history and include, for example, Bourbons, Centifolias, Damasks, Gallicas, Hybrid Musks and Moss roses. There are other shrub types with more modern origins and longer flowering periods. These include the New English roses introduced by David Austin Roses during recent years. Many of these are described and illustrated on pages 106 and 107.

LEFT The climber 'Pink Perpétue' grows up to 2.7m (9ft) high and develops large clusters of pink flowers with a carmine reverse. It was introduced in 1965 from a cross between the climbers 'Danse du Feu' and 'New Dawn'.

ABOVE The Miniature bush rose 'Angela Rippon' creates a wealth of small, double, rosy salmon-pink flowers amid bushy growth and on compact plants about 45cm (1½ ft) high and 30cm (1ft) wide.

RIGHT The Modern Shrub rose 'Rosy Cushion' forms a shrub about 75cm (2½ ft) high and 1.5m (5ft) wide, packed with small, single, pink flowers. Each flower reveals a white heart.

USING AND DISPLAYING ROSES

There are few places in a garden, however small, that cannot be enhanced by roses. Ground-cover types brighten the soil with flowers, pillar roses stand like sentries and create colour throughout much of summer, standard roses introduce height into rose beds, while miniature and patio types can be introduced into even the smallest area of courtyard or balcony. Climbers and Ramblers cover walls and fences, some scaling lofty trees.

Roses have great scope beyond the garden in indoor arrangements, in bouquets and buttonholes. In the kitchen the fruits, known as hips, can be used in rose-hip jam and rose honey and the petals can be crystallized or used in rose vinegar. Both petals and hips can be used in the making of wine.

VERSATILE ROSES

In earlier times, bush roses were usually planted in formal beds on their own and not integrated with the rest of the garden. Nowadays, shrub roses are being planted in shrub borders, while tall varieties of Hybrid Teas and Floribundas are quite at home in borders alongside herbaceous plants and shrubs. There is also a trend to plant low-growing plants under bush roses to create colour when the roses are not at their best. Ground-cover roses, with their prostrate but not weed-suppressing nature, are ideal for camouflaging manhole covers, covering banks too steep to grass and mow, and filling planting areas left in patios. But, unless the area is large, choose a variety of only moderate vigour.

Increasingly, roses are being grown in tubs on patios, in window boxes and even in hanging baskets. But not all varieties are suitable for such places and care is needed to ensure the compost does not dry out or that the foliage is not exposed to leaf-burning cold draughts.

Hedges are another effective way to grow roses, forming colourful barriers 1.5m (5ft) or more tall; others are miniature and 75cm (2½ft) or less high.

ABOVE The Rambler 'Violette' produces clusters of small, crimson-purple flowers that fade to maroon. It grows to about 4.5m (15ft) high and is ideal for clothing an arch. It is a beautiful Multiflora Rambler and forms an eye-catching display.

LEFT A bed packed with bush roses creates a colour-packed feature. This bed uses mass planting of roses of different types and sizes, from front to back: 'Hakuun' (Patio rose) with buff to creamy-white flowers; 'Indian Summer' (Hybrid Tea) with creamy-orange blooms; 'Fountain' (Modern Shrub rose) with bright-crimson heads.

ABOVE The Bourbon Climber 'Blairi No. 2' grows about 4.5m (15ft) high and creates a wealth of cupped, full-petalled, deep-pink flowers which pale towards the edges. It was raised in 1845 and is excellent as a pillar rose or trained against a wall. It has the bonus of bearing mahogany-tinted foliage and creates a spectacular shrub.

RIGHT Mixing roses with shrubs and herbaceous perennials creates fascinating combinations of colour and shape, producing harmonies reminiscent of cottage gardens. This path is flanked with a medley of climbing and Shrub roses: the deep-pink Climbers, 'Blairii No. 2' (right front), the pale-pink Bourbon rose, 'Mme Lauriol de Barny' (right back), the lilac-pink Bourbon rose, 'Louise Odier' (left front), and the blush-pink Scotch rose, 'Stanwell Perpetual' (left back). At the front is the herbaceous *Polemonium caeruleum*.

ABOVE 'Raubritter', a Modern Shrub rose, is ideal both as a border edging and to smother the ground in flowers and foliage. It sprawls to form a low mound and develops large, freely borne clusters of slightly fragrant pink flowers. This shrub grows about 90cm (3ft) high and 1.5m (5ft) wide.

ABOVE Planting roses in combination with shrubs and herbaceous plants creates a feature which keeps its interest over a long period. Do not mix these different plants in rigid, formal rows; instead, create an informal outline so that they all merge together and look totally natural.

ABOVE Many Miniature roses are ideal for containers positioned on patios and balconies, or for planting in window boxes. They flower almost continually and create colour for many months during summer. There are many varieties to choose from and in a wide range of colours.

THE ENVIRONMENT
Choosing and improving

Roses are hardy, tolerant shrubs that will grow in most soils and environments, but to get the best from them some care is necessary. Choose an open, bright, sunny site, preferably lightly shaded in the afternoon. Air should be able to circulate between the stems and leaves. Do not plant roses under trees, where water can drip on them long after the rain has stopped. Avoid draughty places between buildings, as they are often sunless with dry soil, and where the wind will rapidly dry the foliage. Some roses will grow against a north-facing wall, but shelter from cold winds is usually advisable. In windy and exposed areas, plant roses in the lee – but not shade – of a hedge. Avoid positions at the base of slopes where frost collects, or on the sides of slopes where frost can be trapped (*see far right*). Well-drained soil is essential to prevent roots decaying, especially in heavy, compacted clay. Therefore, break up the subsoil and install drains (*see below*).

Selecting a site
When selecting a site for roses, avoid cold areas, especially where freezing air travels downhill and accumulates so that plants become entirely covered. Tall hedges at the base of slopes cause cold air to become trapped (see above).

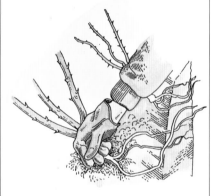

HOW TO MAKE SOIL MORE ALKALINE

The amount of lime needed to raise the pH (decrease the acidity) depends on the form in which it is applied and on the type of soil. As a guide, the following amounts of lime should decrease acidity by about 1.0 pH. For roses, a slightly acid soil is desirable, with a pH of 6.0–6.5.

Kits to assess acidity or alkalinity are widely available. Some rely on chemicals, others have a probe with the pH reading indicated on a dial (an ideal method if you are red–green colour-blind).

Soil	Hydrated lime	Ground limestone
Clay	610g/sq m (18oz/sq yd)	810g/sq m (24oz/sq yd)
Loam	410g/sq m (12oz/sq yd)	540g/sq m (16oz/sq yd)
Sand	200g/sq m (6oz/sq yd)	270g/sq m (8oz/sq yd)

'Heeling in' a rose
When roses are bought as bare-rooted plants from a nursery they will arrive anytime between late autumn and late winter, when they are dormant. If the soil is not frozen or waterlogged, plant them immediately, but if the ground is unfit they must be 'heeled in'. This involves digging a trench about 25cm (10in) deep and with one side sloping at 45 degrees. Choose a sheltered corner. Place the roots in it and cover them with soil (above). Lightly firm the soil so that the roots do not become dry.

DRAINAGE

Clay pipe drains are laid in a herring-bone fashion with their ends butted together and the joints covered.

Rubble drains are cheaper than clay pipes, but trenches still have to be dug and sloped towards a sump.

Continuous plastic drains are a more modern development, quicker and easier to install, especially in clay soil.

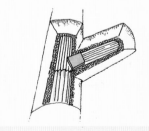

BUYING ROSES

Unless plants are healthy when bought they will never grow satisfactorily. Do not be tempted to buy cheap, inferior plants and always check them before buying or as soon as they arrive by mail or carrier from a nursery. Bare-rooted varieties are usually ordered through catalogues issued by rose nurseries; the roses are often illustrated but for a better idea of what they are like visit an established rose garden and see them growing. Pre-packed roses often have a coloured illustration of the flowers on their packaging. With this kind of presentation, there is a risk that plants can become excessively warm, initiating growth or encouraging diseases. Container-grown roses are available from garden centres and a car is necessary to get them home, but some garden centres have a delivery service.

EXISTING ROSES

If you move to an established garden it is possible it will have several established roses. If they are old and neglected, with masses of thin, spindly shoots and thick, knotted bases to their stems, they are best removed and replaced with fresh plants. It is advisable to improve the soil before planting these new roses.

If the established roses were not infested with diseases, it is enough just to check that the drainage is satisfactory and to plant a young rose bush with a couple of buckets of fresh compost around its roots. However, if the roses were diseased, either select a fresh area or replace most of the soil with fresh compost. Check that the subsoil is well drained.

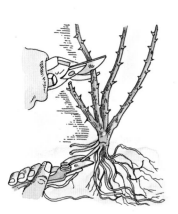

ABOVE As soon as the soil is not frozen or waterlogged, prepare bare-rooted rose bushes for planting. Cut off old leaves, hips and thin, weak shoots growing from the main branches. Cut back long or damaged roots to about 30cm (12in) long. Pre-packed roses must be treated in the same way.

ABOVE To ensure the roots and stems are plump and not shrivelled when the bush is planted, place them in a bucket deeply filled with water. Ensure the bases of the main branches are also immersed. This especially applies to pre-packed roses. Leave them to soak in the water overnight.

WHEN BUYING ROSES

There are three main forms in which roses can be bought: 'bare-rooted', 'pre-packed' and 'container-grown'. Each of these has advantages and disadvantages, and the first two forms are available only at certain times of the year.

Bare-rooted: These are grown in nurseries, dug up during their dormant period (from late autumn to late winter) and sold either direct or through mail order. Avoid plants with dry stems or roots.

Pre-packed: Plants are dug up in their dormant state, their roots covered with moist peat and the entire plant wrapped in polythene. Unfortunately, this encourages premature growth if kept too warm.

Container-grown: Plants are grown in containers and can be sold throughout the year. Check that the compost in the container is not excessively dry or wet, and that the plant is not pot-bound.

PLANTING ROSES

Gardeners with decades of experience will remember bare-rooted roses arriving from nurseries, packed in pyramidal straw bundles and tied with string. Nowadays, plants often arrive in large, multi-layer paper sacks, which are closed by machine stitching. The passing of the old method is mourned by many gardeners, but new ways cut costs and save time. It also ensures that straw is not scattered everywhere.

When bare-rooted plants arrive, leave the package unopened if planting is possible within seven days. Store them meanwhile in a cellar or cool, vermin-free shed or garage. If planting is impossible within seven days, because of the freezing weather or waterlogged or frozen soil, remove the packaging and heel in their roots (*see page 12*). For pre-packaged roses, remove the polythene immediately and either cover with sacking and place in a cellar or cool shed, or heel in. Container-grown plants, if they cannot be planted immediately, should be placed in a cool, wind- and sun-sheltered corner and the compost kept moist but not waterlogged. Always check that the bush is labelled. Re-secure those that are loose as once a label is lost it may be difficult to identify the plant.

BARE-ROOTED ROSES

Most roses are planted with their roots bare of soil, although container-grown types are increasing in popularity. Pre-packaged roses – which tend to be impulse buys from high-street shops and supermarkets, as well as garden centres – are prepared and planted in the same way as bare-rooted types.

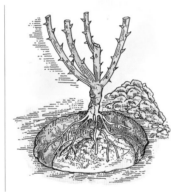

1 Plant a bare-rooted rose from late autumn to late winter. Dig a hole 50–60cm (20–24in) wide and 20–25cm (8–10in) deep. Fill the base with equal parts good soil and moist peat, plus a sprinkling of bonemeal, then form and firm a mound (*left*).

3 Work a mixture of equal parts good soil and moist peat, plus a sprinkling of bonemeal, between the roots. Ensure air pockets do not remain around them. Sharply lifting and lowering the rose's stem several times helps to ensure the roots and soil are in close contact. Firm further compost in layers around the roots, using the heel of a shoe (*above*). Do not completely fill the hole with soil, then firm it and after the bush has been planted, use a garden fork to level the soil. If footprints are left on the surface they may form puddles of water later.

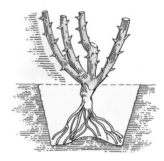

2 Place the bush in the hole and spread the roots over the mound. Check that the join just below the lowest stem, between the variety and rootstock, is about 2.5cm (1in) below the surface when planting is complete (*above*). This allows for soil settlement.

MOVING ESTABLISHED ROSES

It is easier to buy a new bush rose than to move an old, established specimen. But there are times when, due to its rarity or because it was bought to commemorate a special occasion such as a wedding, it is sometimes worth moving an established bush. Tackle the job in late autumn or early spring. First, shorten the branches and then dig down and under the roots. Slide the roots – and as much soil as possible – on to a strong sack and gently carry or slide it to a new hole. Plant it firmly, then water the soil thoroughly.

CONTAINER-GROWN ROSES

Less root disturbance is caused to container-grown roses than to bare-rooted and pre-packaged types. They are therefore able to continue growing unchecked and are ideal for creating 'instant' rose borders and beds.

1 When planting a container-grown rose bush, first check that the compost is moist. This may mean thoroughly watering the compost two or three times during the preceding couple of days (*above*).

2 Dig a hole 38–45cm (15–18in) wide and 25cm (10in) deep. Fork the base, firm it and add a 5cm (2in) thick mixture of equal parts good soil and moist peat, plus a sprinkling of bonemeal. Place the container on top, check that its top is level with the surrounding soil and then carefully remove the container (*above*). Firm soil and peat around the root-ball, in layers.

STANDARD ROSES

These need firm planting and a stout stake to ensure strong winds cannot blow them over and snap off the stem. Lightly clipping off long shoots when they are planted helps to reduce the area buffeted by wind, especially in exposed areas. Later, these roses can be properly pruned (*see pages 26 and 27*).

If standard and bush roses are to be planted in the same border, plant the standard ones first. It is then easier to space out and plant bush types around them.

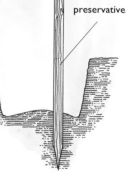

RIGHT Positioning the stake on the windward side of the stem prevents the two rubbing and the stem becoming damaged.

Treat the lower 60cm (2ft) of the stake with a plant-friendly wood preservative.

1 When planting a standard, half-standard or weeping standard rose, form a hole 50–60cm (20–24in) wide and 25cm (10in) deep. Fork over the base and firm the soil. Then, drive a stout stake – slightly off-centre and towards the prevailing wind – 45cm (18in) into the soil (*above*). Spread a 5cm (2in) thick layer of equal parts soil and moist peat, plus a sprinkling of bone-meal, over the base of the hole.

RIGHT If an upper layer of roots is present, cut them off.

Ensure the stake is upright and firmly in the ground.

2 Form and firm a small mound of good soil and moist peat in the base of the hole and position the plant on top (*above*). Check that the soil mark (dark area) on the stem is 12–25mm ($\frac{1}{2}$–1in) deeper than before; this allows for later settlement of the soil. Position the stem on the lee side of the stake, spread out the roots, then work and firm soil over them in thin layers. Ensure the soil and roots are in close contact so that rapid establishment is possible. When the soil is level and firmed, lightly rake the surface to remove footmarks.

Position the top tree-tie about 2.5cm (1in) below the top of the stake.

Lightly cut back the branches.

3 Check that the top of the stake is about 2.5cm (1in) below the lowest branch. Loosely fit three tree-ties: at the top, 23cm (9in) above the ground, and one between them. (*above*). Re-check and secure them about four weeks later, after soil settlement.

SPACING BUSH AND STANDARD ROSES

The distances recommended here are between plants with a similar habit. The spacings indicated for bush roses allow their foliage to touch or overlap slightly. Therefore, when planting them near to the edge of a border, allow a slightly greater distance.

Miniature roses	30cm (12in)
Patio roses	30–38cm (12–15in)
Hybrid Tea/Floribunda	
(compact and small)	45–60cm (1$\frac{1}{2}$–2ft)
(average growth)	60–75cm (2–2$\frac{1}{2}$ft)
(vigorous and tall)	75cm–1m (2$\frac{1}{2}$–3$\frac{1}{2}$ft)
Standard and half-standard	1.2–1.5m (4–5ft)
Weeping standard	1.8m (6ft)

LOOKING AFTER ROSES

Unlike many other deciduous shrubs, which need only yearly pruning and feeding, roses require extra attention to encourage rapid growth and the development of large, shapely flowers. Pruning is explained on pages 24 to 27 and there are tasks such as hoeing, weeding, mulching, removing suckers and dead-heading. Feeding is a major job that should not be neglected. But plants must not be fed late in the season as this encourages the development of sappy growth that will not mature and harden by the onset of cold weather in autumn and early winter. Soft growth is more likely to become diseased than healthy, firm shoots.

PESTS AND DISEASES
These are a continual problem and especially when the same plants are grown in a group. Whenever you are working on roses, check the buds and leaves for any signs of an attack. A range of problems is detailed on pages 20 and 21.

REGULAR ATTENTION

Looking after roses is not an onerous task and most rose enthusiasts are constantly looking for reasons to inspect and admire their plants, both during the early part of the year when shoots are developing, as well as when the flowers start to open. These jobs include watering plants during droughts, removing suckers and disbudding to encourage large blooms.

Shoots known as suckers often grow from the roots of budded rose bushes. They arise from below soil level and have leaves differently coloured and shaped from the main plant. As soon as they appear, use a trowel to move soil from around the sucker's base. Then, with a downward tug, pull it off (*above*). Do not use a knife or secateurs.

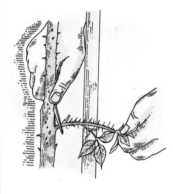

Standard roses sometimes have suckers growing from their roots. Remove them in the same way as for bush roses. Suckers growing on stems can be removed when young by rubbing them sideways (*above*). If they are long, use a sharp knife; cut flush with the stem.

Watering is not usually needed once the plant has established itself and during normal seasons. But much depends on the nature of the soil. If it is light and sandy, regular watering is essential. Newly planted roses also need regular watering. When applying water, do not just dampen the surface but thoroughly saturate the soil and continue doing so until there is an appreciable rainfall.

Replacing poor soil

Where roses have continually been grown in the same soil for a decade or more, it is likely that the soil, unless regularly fed and annually mulched, will be exhausted and the quality of the flowers and plants will deteriorate. If this happens, remove the old soil and replace it with fresh topsoil before replanting new roses in places vacated by old ones.

From mid-spring and throughout summer, shallowly hoe around roses to eradicate weeds (*above*), but take care not to damage roots as this encourages the development of suckers. Do not hoe deeper than 2.5cm (1in) and try to create a fine tilth (a layer of thin, friable soil) on the surface as this reduces the loss of moisture from the ground.

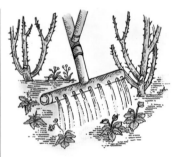

Weed-killing chemicals can be used between rose bushes and standards to kill weeds. Use a dribble-bar attached to a watering-can to apply the chemical evenly (*above*). Wear gloves and thoroughly clean the equipment after use.

When selecting roses for room decoration, cut from established bushes without spoiling the shape of the bush. Choose strong stems, cutting off not more than a third of their length, and severing just above a leaf-joint.

FEEDING ROSES

Each year, bush roses are dramatically pruned to encourage the development of strong, fresh shoots. It is therefore essential that the plants are regularly fed with a fertilizer containing the major plant foods (nitrogen, phosphate and potash) as well as others which are needed in smaller amounts (calcium and magnesium) and those where only a trace is needed (iron, boron and manganese). These are applied in three main ways:

* Powder or granular: These are the traditional – and still widely used – ways to apply plant foods. Sprinkle fertilizer around plants in spring (slightly before the leaves are fully open), again in early summer and a further application in mid-summer. Do not feed after this date. If a mulch has been applied after the first application, continue with a liquid fertilizer.

* Liquid fertilizers: Concentrated liquid fertilizer is diluted and watered on the soil around plants. As long as the soil is moist, plants respond rapidly and develop fresh growth. From mid-spring to the latter part of mid-summer, make applications of the fertilizer every five weeks.

* Foliar sprays: These are sprays of diluted fertilizers that are applied directly onto the the plant foliage. Rose bushes respond rapidly to this type of treatment, and it is used especially for invigorating roses that are being grown for exhibition. Apply foliar sprays that are made by diluting fertilizer in clean water onto plant foliage every month from mid-spring to the end of mid-summer .

1 Start feeding roses in spring, just before the leaves are fully open. Shallowly hoe the surface, then lightly dust it with a granular fertilizer.

2 Lightly hoe the fertilizer into the surface soil, but not more than 2.5cm (1in) deep. Then, thoroughly water the area, taking care not disturb or wash away the surface soil.

3 Then form a 5–7.5cm (2–3in) thick layer of well-decayed organic material such as garden compost over the soil, but not too close to the stems (*see above*). Mulches help to prevent the growth of weeds, provide nutrients for plants and keep the surface soil cool. They also prevent heavy drops of rain splashing off the soil and on to the plants.

Regularly cutting off dead flowers prevents the bush directing its energies into developing seeds rather than growth. It also tidies up the plant. Cut off each dead flower just above a leaf-joint (*above*).

Disbudding encourages the development of large flowers on Hybrid Tea bush roses. Disbud the flowers by snapping off sideways the small buds growing from the leaf-joints immediately below the top bud (*above*). Do this while these secondary buds are still small and can be removed without leaving large scars on the stem.

Throughout summer, Climber, Rambler and pillar roses need to be trained and secured to supports (*above*). Ensure the individual ties are loose enough to allow the stems to thicken. For pillar roses, either tie the stems individually or coil string around them (*right*).

De-shooting, another term for thinning, is performed in spring. Often, two or more shoots develop from a bud. If left, they cause congestion and weak growth. Therefore, all but one bud at each position is left (*below*). Remove the weakest of those facing inwards by carefully bending them sideways until they snap off. However, when very small they can be rubbed off.

FIRMING LOOSE SOIL

Always check the soil around roses in spring; use the heel of your shoe to re-firm all loose soil. This especially applies to bare-rooted roses planted in early winter. If this task is neglected, the roots do not become established.

INCREASING ROSES

By far the most popular way to increase roses is by budding. This is when a bud of the desired variety is merged with a rootstock of known vigour and characteristics. Budding especially applies to Hybrid Tea and Floribunda roses. There are three other methods of increasing roses: by cuttings, seeds and layering. Ramblers, Climbers, most Shrub types and Floribundas with a vigorous nature can be increased from cuttings. Miniature types are also propagated from cuttings, while layering is an excellent method of increasing roses with long, pliable stems, such as Wichuraiana and Multiflora Ramblers and some Shrub roses like the Hybrid Musks. Layering is performed in mid- and late summer; cut a small tongue in the underside of a long shoot and 30–45cm (12–18in) from its end. Hold the tongue open with a twig and bury it (still attached to the parent plant) about 7.5cm (3in) deep. Sowing seeds is another method and is detailed on the opposite page.

ROOTSTOCKS

Commercially, rootstocks are planted 30–38cm (12–15in) apart in early autumn.

• Seedling briar (*Rosa canina*): Raised from seeds and more than 80% of all roses are budded on it.

• Cutting briar (*R. canina*): Raised from cuttings. Not widely used for bush roses but excellent for standards.

• Rugosa (*R. rugosa*): Raised from cuttings and often used for standard roses.

TIMING

Bud roses in mid-summer, as soon as the rind lifts easily from the wood. In hot areas, make the T-cut on the side away from strong sunlight; in other areas, on the side towards the prevailing wind so that the ensuing shoot is blown against – and supported by – the rootstock. For bush roses, scrape soil from the rootstock. Make the T-cut 36–50mm (1½–2in) above the ground.

In early spring of the following year, cut the rootstock's stem 12mm (½in) above the budded part.

Budding bush roses

1 Use a trowel to draw soil away from the neck of the rootstock and use a sharp knife to form a T-shaped cut; the horizontal one 18mm (¾in) long and vertically about 36mm (1½in).

2 Use the spatula end of a budding knife to ease open the flaps of the cuts. Hold the bud part by its leaf-stalk and gently slide it under the bark. Push it to the base of the cut.

3 Use a sharp knife to cut off the top of the bud part at the same position as the horizontal cut in the rootstock. Press back the flaps so that they hold the bud part secure and exclude air.

4 Secure the bud with moist raffia – without constricting the stem. After about three weeks the leaf-stalk falls off. If the bud is green, budding has been successful – slit the raffia on the opposite side to the bud.

BUDS FOR BUDDING

Select a healthy shoot, which has just finished flowering, of the desired variety and cut off a piece 25–30cm (10–12in) long.

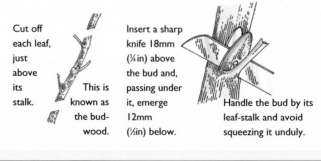

Cut off each leaf, just above its stalk. This is known as the bud-wood.

Insert a sharp knife 18mm (¾in) above the bud and, passing under it, emerge 12mm (½in) below. Handle the bud by its leaf-stalk and avoid squeezing it unduly.

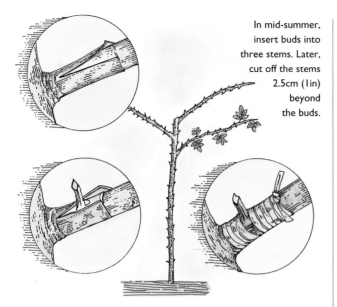

In mid-summer, insert buds into three stems. Later, cut off the stems 2.5cm (1in) beyond the buds.

Standard roses are increased by budding in exactly the same way as for bush types. The only difference is that three (sometimes two) buds are used and inserted at the top of tall rootstocks: half-standards are budded 75cm (2½ft) above the ground, full standards 1m (39in). Prepare rootstocks by allowing a single stem to grow and in late autumn cutting it 15cm (6in) above the desired budding height. Shoots develop and in mid-summer insert buds into two or three of them. Ensure that the buds are not knocked.

Healthy foliage on mature stems produced earlier during the same season. Discard all shoots which have been infested with pests or diseases.

Take cuttings of roses in early or mid-autumn, selecting them from healthy, disease- and pest-free mature shoots of the current year's growth and about the thickness of a pencil. As a judgement of maturity, the thorns should snap off when pushed from the side. Use sharp secateurs to form cuttings about 23cm (9in) long, cleanly severing the stem just above a bud and slightly below a leaf-joint.

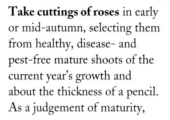

Use a sharp knife to re-check that the stem has been cut just below a leaf-joint and that the bud at its base has not been damaged. Then, dip the base of the cutting in a hormone rooting powder to encourage the rapid formation of roots before it starts to deteriorate and begins to decay.

Choose a sheltered corner, where the soil is moist but not waterlogged, and use a spade to form a trench about 15cm (6in) deep. One of its sides should be vertical, the other about 45 degrees. Sprinkle a 5cm (2in) thick layer of sharp sand in the trench's base and then position the cuttings about 15cm (6in) apart along the vertical side, with their bases pushed into the sand. Refill the trench with friable soil and then firm it with the heel of your shoe. Then, water the soil. In spring, re-firm the soil and throughout summer keep it moist. In late autumn the cuttings can be planted into a nursery-bed or directly into a border.

RAISING ROSES FROM SEEDS

Roses can be raised from seed but for most of them do not expect the progeny to be garden-worthy, especially if you have removed a few hips from a Hybrid Tea or Floribunda type. Indeed, about two or three seedlings out of 20,000 might have some merit! Nevertheless, unless one waits for a natural mutation (called a sport), it is the only way to produce new varieties of roses.

Several seed companies sell seeds of species types and these range from the Alpine rose (*Rosa alpina*) to eglantine (*R. rubiginosa*). Also, the seeds of Miniature roses such as *R. polyantha* are available. When saving your own seeds, gather hips in autumn and store them in a dry, cool box. Remove them in early spring, when the pulpy covering will have decayed. Rub them between your hands to separate the seeds and sow about 12mm (½in) deep in pots of soil-based compost. Place them outdoors in a shaded corner. After germination, plant the seedlings in individual small pots.

PROBLEMS WITH ROSES

Pests, diseases and growth problems are likely to occur from time to time in the life of the rose. Plants are less vulnerable to pest and disease problems if they are grown strongly and given a balanced diet of nitrogen, phosphates and potash. However, plants in soil which is excessively rich in nitrogen have soft leaves and stems and as a result are often more susceptible to diseases.

The range of chemicals available for killing pests and controlling diseases is wide and every year new ones are introduced or re-formulated, while stricter safety regulations frequently preclude the use of old and, perhaps, trusted methods. Whatever the chemical selected, always read the instructions on the label before using it and closely follow them – for example, do not make the mixture stronger or weaker. Always spray during an evening when there is little wind, the sky is cloudy and the sunlight dull. The plant must be dry.

PLANT FOOD DEFICIENCIES

These are indicated by changes in shape and colour of leaves; sometimes yellowing, occasionally becoming smaller and darker. However, do not confuse these colour changes with those that happen naturally in autumn.

Rose rust is not a common problem but should it occur in their first year plants might die. Small, rust-coloured swellings appear on the under-surface of leaves, later turning black. Undernourished plants, cold springs and dry summers encourage an attack. Burn severely infected plants and, as a preventative, spray with a rust-controlling fungicide every two weeks.

Die back is caused by a fungus which gains entry through wounds in stems or from pruning cuts. Decay begins and quickly spreads both up and down the stem, causing blackening. Leaves turn yellow and fall prematurely and if the disease is neglected the whole plant dies. Dig up and burn seriously infected bushes or cut out infected parts. Feed plants well during summer.

Balling is a cultural problem; flower buds fail to open, turn brown and decay. Balling is not likely to occur on well-grown rose bushes, but is caused by wet summers. Also, large, thin-petalled flowers have a tendency to ball. Make sure plants are well fed.

Mildew is a common disease of roses and in wet seasons may assume epidemic proportions. In dry years it is seldom seen, but cold nights and warm days encourage it. Small, grey or white spots cover leaves and buds, sometimes causing them to fall off. Spray repeatedly with a proprietary fungicide.

Black spot is a notorious, serious and common disease of roses. It is a fungal disease that creates black spots on leaves. It becomes very noticeable in mid- and late summer, but it starts in spring when spores create small, black specks. Soils rich in nitrogen and lacking potash encourage it, as does warm and wet weather. Spray regularly in spring and summer. And pick up and burn all prunings.

SPRAY PROGRAMME

Regularly spraying plants helps to control pests and diseases. Remember that fungicides are intended to prevent, rather than to cure, diseases. Insecticides are invariably applied after an insect's presence is noticed. Some insecticides are systemic, which means that the chemical enters the plant's sap stream. There are also systemic fungicides available.

ROSE PESTS

Roses, like all other garden plants, are likely to become infested with pests at some time during their lives. Regularly inspecting your roses and spraying as soon as signs of attack are seen prevents a minor problem becoming a catastrophe. Some rose experts do not wait for signs of an attack, but spray several times throughout summer – late spring, early summer, mid-summer and late summer – to ensure pest problems never increase to plague proportions.

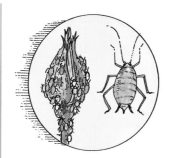

Aphids (greenflies) are common pests, clustering around soft shoots and buds, sucking sap and causing distortion. The aphids excrete honeydew which encourages the presence of sooty mould, an unsightly black fungus. Spray with a systemic insecticide.

Cuckoo-spit is unsightly and contains the yellowish-green nymphs of frog-hoppers. The nymphs suck sap from stems and may cause shoots or buds to wilt. Use a strong jet of clean water to dislodge and remove the spittle, then use a systemic insecticide.

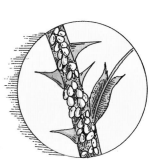

Rose scale forms small, scurfy, crust-like whitish scales which are most often seen on old, neglected bushes. Cut off badly infected stems when pruning. On young parts, the scales can be wiped off with methylated spirits (rubbing alcohol). Alternatively, use an insecticide.

Caterpillars of several moths chew rose leaves and produce irregularly shaped holes. If only a few caterpillars are present, pick them off and destroy. Alternatively, spray with a general insecticide, treating both sides of the leaves. Repeat the spray as necessary

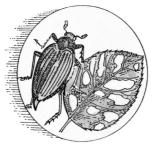

Cockchafer beetles are especially prevalent on light soil. Four types attack roses, including the rose chafer below. The adults fly during early summer, alight on leaves and create irregular shaped holes. Pick off and destroy the beetles, or use an insecticide.

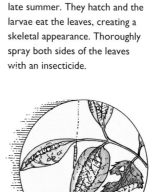

Rose slugworms eat the soft tissue from leaves. Shiny black adult flies lay eggs on leaves in mid- and late summer. They hatch and the larvae eat the leaves, creating a skeletal appearance. Thoroughly spray both sides of the leaves with an insecticide.

Rose leaf-hoppers suck sap from leaves and cause mottling during spring and summer. They usually leave white, cast-off skins on the undersides of leaves. The adults jump about when disturbed. Spray with an insecticide as soon as these pests are seen.

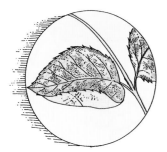

Red spider mites are especially prevalent in hot, dry seasons, when they create bronze patches on the upper surfaces of leaves. The minute, yellowish, eight-legged mites sometimes create fine webbing on leaves. Spray with an insecticide. They are prevalent in mid-summer.

Rose chafer beetles, with bright green wing-case and chest, infest leaves but cause most damage by chewing flowers. Blooms become deformed, often on one side only. Pick off and destroy beetles as soon as they are noticed. Also use an insecticide.

Tortrix moths chew leaves and cause the edges of leaves to roll upwards. Buds and flowers may also be damaged. The moths use silken threads to tie the leaf edges together. Pick off and burn infested leaves and thoroughly spray with an insecticide.

Leaf-rolling sawfly causes leaves to hang downwards, their edges to roll together and eventually to shrivel. The greyish-green sawfly grub is within the rolled leaf. Squeeze rolled leaves to kill grubs and spray the affected bushes with an insecticide.

BUSH ROSES

These are the most popular garden roses and each year many millions of them are sold. The term bush rose refers to Hybrid Teas (now correctly known as Large-flowered roses) and Floribundas (now correctly known as Cluster-flowered roses). Patio roses, Miniature roses and Dwarf Polyanthas are, of course, bush-shaped, but these are usually listed under their own names and not as bush roses.

In recent years, The World Federation of Rose Societies decided that names more applicable and descriptive to Hybrid Tea and Floribunda roses should be introduced, but these have not been enthusiastically received by the general public who, having known the old names, still look for them in rose catalogues. In these circumstances it is not too surprising that nursery catalogues continue to use the old terms. Indeed, even booklets published by The Royal National Rose Society include examples of both the old and new names.

Changing the name of any garden plant and gaining its general acceptance is always likely to be difficult. Three influences are at work in the re-naming of roses: botanical purists, commercial acceptability and, for rose enthusiasts, the change from gardening terms which are widely known and trusted – even loved.

Bush roses usually form the main part of a rose garden. They can be used in beds totally devoted to a single variety, creating dramatic and dominant features. Beds of mixed varieties are also appealing and usually more practical in a small garden than borders totally devoted to one variety. Tall Floribunda types are superb when combined with shrubs in mixed borders.

Traditionalist rose growers may blanch at the idea of mixing roses with different plants, but the practice has now become fashionable and is very attractive. It helps to create combinations of colour and form, and to extend the period when a flower-bed is colourful. In small gardens, interspersing roses with other plants is essential.

When mixing and matching roses, do not forget that

ABOVE 'Glad Tidings', a Floribunda rose, has bright-crimson flowers with high centres in trusses packed with many flowers. It was introduced in 1989 and is superb for planting in beds and borders, as well as forming hedges about 75cm (2½ft) high. In 1989 it was voted 'Rose of the Year'.

Climbers, Ramblers and pillar roses form a superb grouping on their own. As well as creating exciting colour harmonies and contrasts, scented varieties can be used to form an oasis of sweet, heady and desirable fragrances.

In the 1980s, low-growing Floribundas were developed as a separate group and called Patio roses. They grew about 45cm (1½ft) high and created a mass of flowers over a long period. This group is now well established and in this book is featured on pages 72 and 73. Miniature roses, which have an even lower stance and a different origin from Patio roses, are presented on pages 68 to 71. Dwarf Polyanthas are on pages 74 and 75 and, although relatively low-growing like Patio and Miniature roses, have a different heritage.

PRUNING BUSH ROSES

Pruning Hybrid Tea (Large-flowered roses) and Floribundas (Cluster-flowered roses) has acquired an unnecessary mystique, yet it is basically quite simple. They are both deciduous shrubs that produce their best flowers on new shoots grown earlier in the same season. The size and number of new shoots that bush roses develop each year is dictated by the degree of severity with which they are pruned. For example, the greater the severity of pruning (the farther the shoots are cut back) the fewer but stronger will be the shoots that later develop. The influence of 'hard', 'moderate' and 'light' pruning is illustrated on page 25. Other factors that influence the way bush roses are pruned, include the fertility of the soil and the kind of blooms desired – perhaps for showing at an exhibition or just for a spectacular garden display.

MAKING THE RIGHT CUT
Part of the technique of pruning roses is to make clean cuts. This can be achieved by using sharp secateurs that are large enough to cut the stem. Never use small secateurs as they become strained and produce ragged surfaces. Cuts more than 12mm (½in) wide should be painted with a fungicidal wound-paint to aid healing and to prevent the entry of diseases into the wood which might cause shoots to deteriorate and to die.

There are two basic types of secateur: cross-over models (earlier known as parrot type) have two curved blades which cross each other. The anvil model has a sharp blade which cuts when in contact with a strong piece of metal known as an anvil.

Pruning knives are not widely used for pruning now as using them successfully requires many years of experience. Curved saws which cut on the pull stroke enable congested stems to be cut out.

THE CORRECT CUT
The position of a cut in relation to a bud is vital: if made too high it encourages the stem to decay and for die back to occur; if made too low it may damage the bud or leave it unsupported. The perfect cut is 6mm (¼in) above an outward-facing bud.

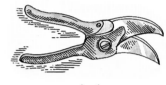
Anvil-type secateurs

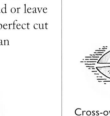
Cross-over secateurs

Grecian saw

Pruning knife

ABOVE The position and slight slant of the above cut is correct.

ABOVE These are examples of the wrong types of pruning cuts: ragged (left) too high (centre) and severing a bud (right).

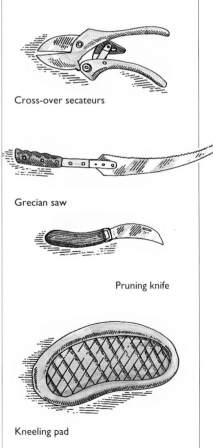
Kneeling pad

WHEN TO PRUNE

Every rose-grower has a particular view about the best time to prune roses, but the general consensus is:

✳ Established bushes, and roses planted in autumn and winter, are best pruned in early spring, just when growth is starting but before leaves appear.

✳ Bushes planted in spring are pruned immediately after planting has been completed.

✳ To prevent bushes being buffeted by winds during winter storms, and their roots becoming loosened in the soil, cut back long stems in early winter. Then, in early spring prune them properly. Always collect up and burn pruned wood.

SOIL AND AGE

The type of soil and age of bushes influence the degree of the severity of pruning. However, always cut out the dead and diseased wood (*right*):

- Hard pruning is ideal for rejuvenating neglected Hybrid Tea types but not suitable for established Floribundas.
- Moderate pruning suits most bush roses, but if Hybrid Tea types become too high and leggy, prune them hard during one season.
- Light pruning is an ideal method for all bush roses growing in sandy soil, which is low in fertility and unable to support the strong growth that comes from hard pruning.

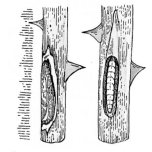  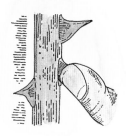

1 First cut out diseased and damaged shoots (*above left*). Cut out shoots infested with the larvae of the shoot borer sawfly (*above right*). Stems with canker can easily be identified by a sunken, brownish or purplish area often surrounded by cracked or flaking bark. These must be cut back to healthy shoots below the cankered area.

2 Next, cut out thin and weak shoots, as well as those which cross the centre of the bush and cause congestion. Such shoots restrict the flow of air through a bush and reduce the amount of light which can enter to ripen the wood in late summer. Cut out shoots which rub against each other, causing damage and the onset of diseases.

3 Cut out unripe stems which, if left, could be damaged by severe winter weather and later introduce diseases into the bush. A test for the maturity of shoots is to snap off several thorns. If they break off cleanly the wood is mature, but if they tear or bend it is a sign of immaturity and that the shoot should be cut back to sound wood.

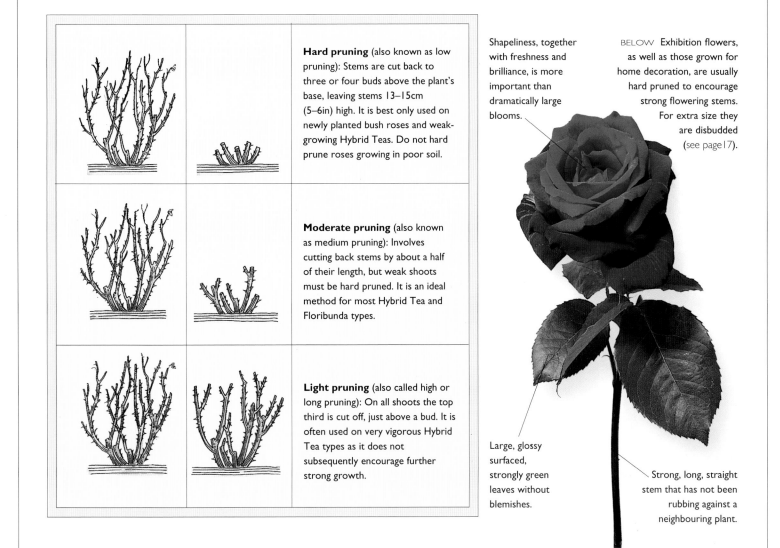

Hard pruning (also known as low pruning): Stems are cut back to three or four buds above the plant's base, leaving stems 13–15cm (5–6in) high. It is best only used on newly planted bush roses and weak-growing Hybrid Teas. Do not hard prune roses growing in poor soil.

Moderate pruning (also known as medium pruning): Involves cutting back stems by about a half of their length, but weak shoots must be hard pruned. It is an ideal method for most Hybrid Tea and Floribunda types.

Light pruning (also called high or long pruning): On all shoots the top third is cut off, just above a bud. It is often used on very vigorous Hybrid Tea types as it does not subsequently encourage further strong growth.

Shapeliness, together with freshness and brilliance, is more important than dramatically large blooms.

BELOW Exhibition flowers, as well as those grown for home decoration, are usually hard pruned to encourage strong flowering stems. For extra size they are disbudded (see page 17).

Large, glossy surfaced, strongly green leaves without blemishes.

Strong, long, straight stem that has not been rubbing against a neighbouring plant.

PRUNING STANDARD AND MINIATURE BUSH ROSES

Standard roses are useful and adaptable: in large gardens they can be planted as centre-pieces in lawns or dotted among bush roses in rose beds, while in small areas they help to make the best use of space, in a similar way to that performed by Climbers and Ramblers. Full standards are better than half-standards or weeping types for planting among other roses. Indeed, it is essential that weeping standards are positioned where their stems can trail unhindered by other plants.

Take care to position standard types where they cannot be buffeted by strong winds, whether in late summer when smothered in flowers and leaves, or in winter when storms are likely to be even more fierce. Tall rose hedges (*see page 78*) are ideal for providing protection against summer winds, although in very exposed areas taller and hardier hedging plants are better, such as conifers.

SINGLE- OR DOUBLE-BUDDED?

The best and most easily managed standard roses have at least two – sometimes three – varietal buds inserted into the top of the rootstock. This ensures that from all angles the standard's head is evenly shaped. However, it is possible that one of these buds will grow more vigorously than the others. If this happens, pruning the weaker shoot more severely will correct the imbalance.

Where only one bud has been used – and it is best not to buy such a plant – it is essential to cut back the ensuing shoot to three or four eyes, so that a strong framework with equally spaced shoots is created. If this task is neglected, the head will never be evenly balanced and create an attractive shape. Also, lop-sided heads are more likely to be damaged by strong winds than those with an even spread of shoots.

Pruning young standard roses

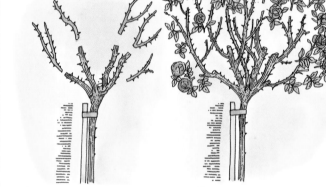

1 Plant bare-rooted standard roses (*see page 14*) during their dormant period, from late autumn to late winter, although standard roses are not usually despatched from nurseries until early or mid-winter. After planting, cut back strong stems to a point 15cm (6in) from the union of the buds at the top of the stem. Pruning this severely encourages the formation of strong branches. It also reduces the area exposed to wind, which otherwise may cause the plant to rock.

2 During the following year, shoots develop which will bear flowers in summer. In mid-autumn or early winter, pruning is necessary. Cut off the tips of stems and cut out immature and soft shoots. Pruning at this stage helps to reduce the area exposed to wind, as well as removing unripe shoots that would not survive winter and might, if left, encourage the onset of decay. At the same time, check that the stake is secure and ties are firm but not too tight.

3 In late winter of the following year, cut out to their base all dead, crossing or weak shoots. Strong loppers may be necessary to ensure a clean and easy cut. Cut out dead and twiggy shoots which are growing from the branches and causing congestion.

4 In late winter, prune back all shoots that developed during the previous year to 15cm (6in) from their base, and lateral shoots to about 10cm (4in) from their point of origin.

Pruning established standard roses

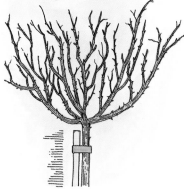

1 Established standard roses need less drastic pruning than when their shape and branches are being formed. Light pruning encourages the development of a large head which can be susceptible to wind damage. When pruning

Hybrid Tea types, cut back strong shoots to about 15cm (6in) from their base. For Floribundas (*above*), cut one-year-old shoots to 23–25cm (9–10in) long, and two-year-old shoots 13–15cm (5–6in) from their base.

Pruning miniature roses

1 Miniature roses have a more twiggy nature than Hybrid Tea or Floribunda roses. In mild areas, prune them in autumn, but in areas of severe winter weather leave pruning until late winter. If pruning is left until winter

remove some of the top growth in autumn to reduce the area exposed to wind. The purpose of pruning is to remove twiggy growth, diseased and damaged shoots, and to create an attractive shape. Cut back vigorous shoots by about a half.

PATIO ROSES

These are low-growing Floribunda roses and can be pruned in the same way as their larger brothers. However, slightly lighter pruning usually suits them best as hard pruning generally encourages the development of fewer blooms and does not produce a mass of flowers.

PRUNING A WEEPING STANDARD

Weeping standards are the 'Victorian ladies' of the world of standard roses; they form weeping crinolines covered with flowers. They are created by inserting several buds at the top of a 130cm (51in) high stem. The result is a head of weeping stems 1.5–1.8m (5–6ft) high. Pruning these roses is quite simple: during late summer or early autumn completely cut out two-year-old shoots that have flowered. This will leave young shoots that developed earlier in the year and will bear flowers during the following year. If there are insufficient young stems to replace the old ones that are cut out, leave a few of them and cut back lateral shoots on them to two or three eyes.

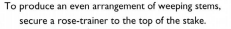

To produce an even arrangement of weeping stems, secure a rose-trainer to the top of the stake.

Always ensure that the stem is well secured in several places to the stake, which must be firmly in the soil.

Rose-trainers are available in several sizes – 60cm (2ft), 75cm (2½ft), and 90cm (3ft) wide.

ABOVE Some ground-cover roses have long, sprawling shoots that eventually smother the ground. Usually, little pruning is needed, as a natural, informal appearance is desired. Where stems intrude on neighbouring plants, prune them to just beyond an upward-facing bud. Where a ground-cover rose has a more upright and shrub-like nature, prune it as a shrub.

HYBRID TEA ROSES

These are widely regarded as the noblest creations of the rose kingdom. Indeed, to many people they are the ideal of what a rose should be. Now properly known as Large-flowered roses, they have long, pointed buds which open to reveal satin-like petals arranged to form a high, central cone. Many are beautifully fragrant. Like Floribunda roses (*see pages 50 to 65*) they can be grown in beds and borders but, unlike them, their flowers are mainly borne singly and not in large sprays, although some do have small clusters of flowers. Their colour range is wide and encompasses most shades although the true blue rose remains elusive. From this page to page 47, Hybrid Tea roses are grouped according to their colours. We begin with white and cream, which bring a cool, calm atmosphere to gardens. Fiery colours such as reds, scarlets and oranges are ideal as 'invigorators', but where a restful setting is desired, nothing equals an ivory or white rose.

MIXING AND MATCHING: WHITE AND CREAM

At one time, mixing roses with other plants would have been thought a total mistake. Nowadays, planting roses in combination with other plants is accepted as an ideal way to provide colour over a longer period. For combinations using white roses try these ideas:

• Underplant the soil between white varieties with the Foam flower (*Tiarella cordifolia*) to create a backcloth of pale to mid-green, maple-shaped leaves. As a bonus it produces spikes of cream-white flowers in early summer.

• Grow low or medium height varieties of white roses against a hedge of lavender: the hedge grows 1–1.2m (3½–4ft) high and when white roses are viewed at an angle and from above they are highlighted by the pale grey-blue flowers of the old English lavender.

RIGHT 'Evening Star' is an American-bred rose, widely grown and popular with large blooms borne singly and in clusters. The lightly scented flowers are shaded yellow at their base. It forms a medium-sized bush about 90cm (3ft) high and 60cm (2ft) wide and develops dark-green, leathery leaves.

'Polar Star' has large, white blooms on strong, upright stems, making it ideal for cutting and indoor decoration. The bush grows about 40cm (28in) high and 1m (3½ft) wide, with large, dark-green leaves.

LEFT 'Westfield Star' is an old
Hybrid Tea-type rose, introduced in
1922, which has superb creamy-
white flowers. It is a sport from
'Ophelia', a 1912 introduction and
is still widely grown and admired.

WHAT IS WHITE?

This is the purest of colours and is seen when all light rays are reflected from the surface upon which they fall. It is bright and clean and reminiscent of newly fallen snow. Few flowers, however, are pure white and most have shades of cream, pink, soft-grey or light lavender. This removes the coldness of white and makes them appear warmer.

White flowers remain bright even as the light fades in evenings, long after reds and even light pinks have melted into darkness. White and cream-flowered roses are therefore ideal for planting in gardens which are mainly visited during summer evenings. Planting them near to patios or at the edges of beds creates beacons that highlight a feature's edge.

The range of Hybrid Tea varieties with white and cream blooms is not wide and few rose enthusiasts would plant beds totally of white roses. Instead, they are mixed and matched with other garden plants (*see opposite page*), either to form contrasts or harmonies.

White Hybrid Tea roses have a formality that does not allow them to be mixed and merged with large herbaceous plants, in the same manner as the shrub-like Species and Old roses. Instead, they usually rely on being underplanted with low-growing herbaceous plants, highlighted by colour-contrasting hedges or mixed in beds with other Hybrid Tea roses.

When white-flowered Hybrid Tea roses are mixed with other roses, ensure that they are not dominated by bold colours such as crimson and scarlet. More white bushes are needed in this setting than if they were being harmonized with soft pink or lavender varieties.

'Pascali' was introduced in 1963 and is still well worth growing. The large, white, long-lasting blooms are more resistant to rain damage than many other white varieties. The scentless flowers, sometimes at first shaded peach, are borne amid tall, upright growth and dark-green leaves which tend to be rather sparse.

OTHER WHITE ROSES TO CONSIDER

* 'Elizabeth Harkness': Ivory blooms, with a touch of pink and gold. It is free-flowering and ideal for bedding and cutting for room decoration.

* 'Peaudouce': Also known as 'Elina', has ivory, moderately scented blooms with a lemon centre. The large, shapely, high-pointed buds open slowly.

* 'Pristine': Large, strongly scented, ivory and blush blooms amid large, dark, handsome leaves.

* 'Virgo': Free-flowering, with large, lightly scented blooms. Unfortunately, the variety is not robust but it is still well worth growing.

YELLOW HYBRID TEAS

This is a very popular colour and several excellent varieties have been introduced during the last decade. Yellow has a way of capturing the attention and in mid- and late summer it recalls the brightness and vitality of spring, when borders were bright with golden daffodils. In addition, yellow is a colour still visible in late evening, long after deep reds and scarlets have been lost in the twilight. Therefore, bushes with flowers this colour are excellent for planting around the edges of patios, at the fronts of borders or by the sides of entrances. Yellow also creates a strong contrast with red or scarlet blooms and is a popular combination.

WHAT IS A YELLOW?

Some rose blooms are clearly yellow, either a dominant, pure and unfading canary-yellow such as 'Freedom' , or light-yellow flowers which show flushes of pink such as 'Grandpa Dickson'. The popular 'Peace' is also light yellow, flushed with pink. Some varieties have yellow flowers verging on orange, while even 'Peaudouce' ('Elina') which has ivory-colour petals but with lemon centres is claimed by some to be a yellow variety rather than a white one. The exact colour shade where orange-yellow becomes yellowish-orange is a personal judgement often influenced by the light intensity at the time.

'Peace' is perhaps the best known of all Hybrid Tea roses. Also known as 'Gloria Dei' and 'Gioia', its large, yellow flowers are flushed pink. The vigorous bushes, often growing 1.2m (4ft) high, should not be hard pruned. Nowadays, 'Peace' appears to be more susceptible to black spot, but nevertheless is still one of the best known and most popular roses.

ABOVE 'Goldstar' develops bright, deep-yellow, unfading flowers on plants with an upright habit. The medium to large flowers are lightly scented. As well as brightening gardens, it is excellent for cutting to display indoors – the flowers are borne on long, straight stems. It is a popular rose and known by several other names, such as 'Candide', 'Goldina' and 'Point du Jour'. In 1984 it won a Gold Medal at The Hague.

LEFT 'Tequila Sunrise' has large, yellow blooms edged in scarlet. These are freely borne amid dark-green leaves.

'Grandpa Dickson' is a superb pale-yellow, lightly scented Hybrid Tea. In hot weather it is flushed with pink. It is also known as 'Irish Gold' and has good resistance to damage from rain. It has a long flowering season and is excellent for planting in beds.

MIXING AND MATCHING

Rich-yellow Hybrid Tea roses are so dominant that they are ideal for creating bold and dramatic colour contrasts. However, yellow is a difficult colour with which to create subtle colour combinations, unless a soft yellow-flavoured rose is chosen. Here are a few companion plantings to try:

* Plant 'Grandpa Dickson' against a strongly coloured background of the rich purple-red-leaved *Berberis thunbergii* 'Atropurpurea', with the addition of the sweetly scented, 60–75cm (2–2½ ft) high flowering tobacco plant *Nicotiana alata* 'Lime Green', which creates a mass of yellow-green flowers throughout the summer.

* A light-yellow rose planted slightly in front of the early-summer flowering golden rain tree (*Laburnum × watereri* 'Vossii' and sometimes also known as *L. × vossii*) creates an attractive arrangement. When combined with a white lilac the display is further enhanced.

* Three red-flowered standard roses planted in a round bed filled with bright-yellow Bush roses creates a bold display, although it may appear too garish to some eyes. An edging of white sweet alyssum (*Lobularia maritima/Alyssum maritimum*) provides a border to hold the display together.

LEFT 'Freedom', also known as 'Dicjem', has rich, bright-yellow petals which do not fade with age and is lightly scented. Bushes have an upright stance with masses of light-green leaves. It is excellent for planting in massed bedding and each year is gaining in popularity.

ABOVE 'Golden Days' creates dominant, deep-yellow blooms amid bushy growth. It is only lightly scented.

OTHER YELLOW HYBRID TEAS

✴ 'Belfast Belle': Large, lightly scented, bright-yellow blooms borne amid upright growth on strongly growing bushes 90cm (3ft) high.

✴ 'Buccaneer': Large, bright-yellow, scented flowers borne in wide clusters on bushes about 1.2m (4ft) high. It used to be a very popular variety.

✴ 'City of Gloucester': Beautiful, lightly scented, saffron-yellow flowers shaded gold. They are large and borne on bushes about 90cm (3ft) high.

✴ 'Diorama': Large, moderately scented, yellow-orange blooms flushed red and borne on branching bushes about 75cm (2½ft) high.

✴ 'Fragrant Gold': Large, well-scented, deep-yellow blooms. Sometimes criticized for the small number of petals, although to many eyes this is a very attractive quality. Bushes grow about 75cm (2½ft) high.

✴ 'Golden Jubilee': Large, lightly scented, yellow blooms touched with pink. They are borne on upright, bushy plants about 90cm (3ft) high.

✴ 'Golden Moments': Lightly scented, amber-yellow blooms amid bushy growth and on plants about 90cm (3ft) high.

✴ 'King's Ransom': Well-established variety, with fragrant, pure-yellow flowers on bushes about 75cm (2½ft) high.

✴ 'Summer Sunshine': Large, moderately scented, bright-yellow blooms on branching bushes. Bushes grow about 75cm (2½ft) high.

✴ 'Sutter's Gold': Well-scented, large, yellow flowers flushed orange and pink. They are borne on upright bushes, about 90cm (3ft) high, but with rather sparse foliage.

ABOVE 'Simba', also known as 'Helmut', 'Goldsmith' and 'Korbelma', creates large, lightly scented, clear-yellow blooms which appear in flushes, rather than continually during summer, on bushes about 60cm (2ft) high. The flowers are resistant to damage from the weather and the stems are firm and strong. The large blooms are prized for their high centres.

RIGHT 'Pot o' Gold', also known as 'Dicdivine', is an outstanding yellow rose, with fragrant blooms. It flowers freely, is weather-resistant and looks good in beds as well as for cutting for room decoration. The flowers are borne in wide sprays on bushy plants about 75cm (2½ft) high.

ABOVE 'Sunblest' has bright-yellow flowers with a light scent. Although the flowers are not large, they are borne prolifically on bushes with an upright stance, about 90cm (3ft) high. Because of its long stems it is an excellent variety for cutting to decorate rooms.

'Super Sun' develops, large, deep-yellow (sometimes classified as orange-shaded), moderately scented blooms on bushes with arching growth. It is a sport of the well-known and widely grown 'Piccadilly'.

'Benson and Hedges Gold' has moderately scented, large, deep-yellow blooms with hints of red. They are borne amid bushy growth.

'Valencia', also known as 'Koreklia', develops large, moderately scented, light amber-yellow blooms amid bushy growth. Bushes grow about 90cm (3ft) high and produce large leaves.

LEFT 'Doris Tysterman' has lightly scented, medium-sized, orange-red blooms sometimes described as tangerine. Bushes have an upright nature, to about 1.2m (4ft), and the glossy, bronze-tinted foliage is slightly susceptible to mildew. The blooms are shapely, excellent for cutting and prized by flower arrangers.

APRICOT, COPPER AND ORANGE HYBRID TEAS

Hybrid Tea roses with these colours are difficult to fit into a precise colour classification. For example, the vermilion-orange 'Cheshire Life' is often put among the oranges, while at other times with the reds. Clearly there is no exact description to suit it.

Apricot, copper and orange are warm but not dominating colours; mixed in flower-beds or planted together en masse they do not have the gaiety of spring yellows nor the glow of vivid reds. When displayed indoors in vases they bring a feeling of warmth to the cool evenings of late summer.

MIXING AND MATCHING

Apricot, copper and orange are not easily combined with other flowers. Being not as bland as white, nor sparking with life like yellow or vivid and dominating like red, they are usually best with flowers of similar colour but different shape and texture.

Indoors, these colours are ideal for displaying in copper containers, with an inner vase used to safeguard the metal. The burnished metal provides a sympathetic setting for rose blooms of these colours.

When arranged, these colours often look better in an old setting than in futuristic and modern surroundings.

'Royal Romance' introduced in 1981, produces medium-sized, fragrant blooms variously described as salmon-peach or salmon-peach with a hint of orange. They are borne on bushy, vigorous bushes about 75cm (2½ ft) high and each flower has about thirty petals.

'Lovers' Meeting' develops wide sprays of reddish-orange blooms on strong, branching bushes.

LEFT 'Just Joey' develops fragrant, large, coppery-orange blooms that pale towards their edges. Its rich colouring has made it a popular variety both in garden beds and as a cut-flower for indoor display. Bushes have a branching nature, up to 75cm (2½ft) high, with dark but sparse foliage.

OTHER APRICOT, COPPER AND ORANGE ROSES TO CONSIDER

✳ 'Adolf Horstmann': Fragrant, orange-yellow blooms with pink edges. The growth is upright and forms very attractive bushes 90cm (3ft) high.

✳ 'Beaut': Large, moderately scented, apricot-orange blooms on moderately vigorous, branching bushes up to 75cm (2½ft) high.

✳ 'Can Can': Large, fragrant, deep orange-scarlet blooms on bushy plants up to 60cm (2ft) high.

✳ 'Champion': Very fragrant, cream or gold flushed red and pink borne on bushy plants up to 60cm (2ft) high. This rose has also been described as primrose-yellow flushed pink.

✳ 'Chicago Peace': Large, slightly fragrant blooms formed of pink, copper and yellow. Bushes are vigorous and shrubby, up to 1m (3½ft) high.

✳ 'Fulton Mackay': Moderately scented, golden-apricot blooms borne on plants about 75cm (2½ft) high.

✳ 'Johnnie Walker': Large, sweetly scented, apricot-coloured blooms on upright and branching bushes over 1m (3½ft) high. It is a very hardy rose.

✳ 'Julia's Rose': Lightly scented orange-salmon blooms borne on bushes slightly more than 60cm (2ft) high. It is an excellent rose to use in flower arrangements.

✳ 'Lincoln Cathedral': Large, lightly scented, deep-pink blooms with orange and gold. Bushes are vigorous and upright, to about 90cm (3ft).

'Cheshire Life' is usually described as orange, but occasionally orange-red and vermilion-orange. The moderately scented, large blooms open in clusters on bushes about 75cm (2½ft) high. It has the virtue of being resistant to diseases.

RIGHT 'Vital Spark' creates a mass of orange-yellow and fiery-red blooms in large clusters on bushes about 90cm (3ft) high and 60cm (2ft) wide. Unfortunately, it is only slightly scented. It has a medley of well-known varieties in its parentage, including 'Anne Cocker' and 'Yellow Pages'.

BELOW 'Rosemary Harkness' has sweetly fragrant, medium-sized, orange-yellow blooms blended with salmon. Bushes are well branched and shrubby and slightly more than 75cm (2½ft) high. When planted en masse in beds it creates a wonderful display. It is also suitable for planting as a hedge.

ABOVE 'Dawn Chorus' was acclaimed Rose of the Year and Breeder's Choice in 1993. It develops masses of exquisitely formed, slightly scented, glowing-orange flowers with yellow at the base of the petals. Each flower has a high centre. Bushes are about 90cm (3ft) high and it is an ideal variety for planting in beds in gardens. It is also superb when planted to form a hedge.

'Whisky Mac' has an unusual name and a strong unusual scent. Its large golden-apricot blooms are a unique colour. Bushes grow about 75cm (2½–3ft) high. To encourage strong growth it must be planted in fertile soil.

RANGE OF COLOURS

Of all Hybrid Tea rose colours, the grouping of apricot, copper and orange is the most extensive; even the popular red does not exceed them in number. This, of course, is because these colours extend across a wide spectrum and are open to a range of opinions about their true colour. They are not piercing and fiery like reds, nor clear and bright like yellow, but warm and comforting like the colours in an autumn fire. Roses of these colours appear mainly during mid-summer and follow the oranges of tulips in late spring and early summer. Orange, copper and apricot roses are therefore ideal for continuing an orange theme until late summer.

Some gardens are famous for their white borders, others for blue themes and this type of garden planning was advocated by the famous English garden designer Gertrude Jekyll (1843–1932). She was mainly concerned with herbaceous perennials, hardy annuals and half-hardy annuals and frequently backed an orange theme with a hedge of yew. Although few modern gardens are large enough to enable the creation of several distinctive colour themes, a small bed entirely devoted to apricot, copper and orange roses is possible, with graduations of colour from light shades at the front to darker ones behind.

'Troika' has large, moderately scented, reddish-orange blooms with yellow and pink. The colours do not fade with age. Bushes grow to about 90cm (3ft) high and are ideal for planting in beds. Its long stems and shapely buds make it ideal for cutting and displaying indoors.

FURTHER APRICOT, COPPER AND ORANGE ROSES

✳ 'Mojave': Slightly fragrant, deep-orange flowers attractively veined in red. These are borne on vigorous, upright bushes about 90cm (3ft) high.

✳ 'L'Oréal Trophy': Lightly scented, large, bright orange-salmon blooms on upright bushes about 1.2m (4ft) high.

✳ 'Remember Me': Fragrant, large, coppery-orange blooms with blends of yellow borne in wide sprays. Bushes grow 90cm (3ft) high.

✳ 'The Lady': Fragrant, large, honey-yellow blooms edged in salmon and borne in wide sprays. The bushes have upright growth, to about 90cm (3ft).

RIGHT 'Lovely Lady' is a superb Hybrid Tea rose, with large rose-pink blooms. Flowers borne amid bushy growth. One of its parents is the well-known 'Silver Jubilee'.

'Paul Shirville' has large, very fragrant, soft salmon-pink blooms with a peach-coloured base. It is justifiably a popular pink, with flowers sometimes reaching the size of dinner plates. Bushes grow about 75cm (2½ft) high and as well as being superb in beds in gardens the flowers are excellent in flower arrangements indoors.

PINK AND BLUSH HYBRID TEAS

Pink is an all-embracing term and includes a wide spectrum of colour, from pinkish-white to light red. Between these shades there is the true classical pink which is demure but has an immediate and quickly perceived warmth and charm.

The strength and richness of pink in blooms is not always essential for popularity; 'Paul Shirville', for example, has only a light salmon-pink tone, but is one of the most popular of all pink Hybrid Tea roses. On the other hand, 'Pink Peace' is strongly pink and that, too, is popular; it is a rose that has won many awards from rose societies in both North America and Britain.

There is no certain recipe for success for rose-breeders when raising a new pink variety. However, part of a rose's success is often the bush's nature, its vigour, ability to flower over a long period and its resistance to weather damage. Some are even resistant to diseases such as mildew and black spot. Pink roses – like red ones – have romantic associations and for this reason alone are well worth growing.

MIXING AND MATCHING

The delicate and demure nature of pink roses can soon be destroyed if plants with colours that dominate or clash with them are planted too close to it.

Pink is often associated with red, which in its totally colour-saturated state is markedly dissimilar to light pink. When light intensity is low in evenings, red can appear black, while light pink still remains visible. Pink is better associated with mauve, a related colour: both have a soft and pleasing cottage-garden style. Pink and mauve are friendly colours and should not be associated with fiery and hostile dark reds and violets.

LEFT 'Blessings' is widely admired and often said to be the ideal rose for planting in beds in gardens. The large, moderately scented, salmon-pink blooms are borne on vigorous, upright bushes, sometimes 1.5m (5ft) high. The blooms, also described as coral-pink, appear in clusters from early in the rose season to late autumn. Do not position other strong-coloured roses too close.

LEFT 'Typhoon' creates a spectacular display of large pink to salmon blooms on leafy bushes about 75cm (2½ ft) high.

'Pink Favourite', a North American variety, has large, slightly fragrant, deep-pink blooms and is ideal for planting in beds in gardens. The high-centred blooms appear later in the rose season than most varieties. The foliage is handsome and the bushes about 75cm (2½ ft) tall.

ABOVE 'Pink Peace' bears large, fragrant, deep-pink blooms on bushes with vigorous, upright growth. The bushes often grow more than 1m (3½ ft) high. The dark-green, leathery leaves make an attractive foil to the flowers.

Pink – as well as mauve – is quickly subdued by strong colours and, therefore, the best partners for them are other cottage-garden plants. These range from lightly shaded white (pure white tends to capture attention and then to retain it), through silver to light greens and pale yellow. Strongly yellow flowers are too dominant, but those with light shades such as lemon – when used sparingly – are excellent collaborators with pink. Combinations of plants to try include:

• A border edging of the herbaceous perennial lamb's tongue (*Stachys byzantina*, better known as *S. olympica and S. lanata*), with tongue-like leaves smothered in a mass of silvery hairs, creates a superb ground-level colour harmony for pink roses.

• The herbaceous perennial catmint (*Nepeta × faassenii*), with whorls of lavender-blue flowers, grows 30–45cm (12–18in) high and can be used as an edging for pink roses. In beds planted with tall, pink-flowered varieties, the catmint can be planted between the roses. When planning this, allow slightly more space between the bushes.

• For a light-green and dark-pink arrangement use a border edging of the herbaceous perennial lady's mantle (*Alchemilla mollis*). This has light-green, hairy, maple-like leaves on plants 30–45cm (12–18in) high. If the path is formed of paving stones or gravel, allow the leaves to spill over so that the entire edging is softened. A strongly pink variety, such as 'Pink Peace', is a good collaborator.

• For a sulphur-yellow backdrop to strongly pink roses try the herbaceous mullein (*Verbascum bombyciferum*). It grows 1.2–1.8m (4–6ft) high and during mid-summer produces tall spikes of flowers. But do not select verbascums with strongly yellow flowers.

CUT-FLOWER DISPLAYS

Many can also be used in flower arrangements indoors. Fresh roses look superb on their own, especially romantic pink ones. Even the gift of a single rose is a memorable treasure to the recipient.

When displaying them indoors, carefully select a vase to complement the flowers. Pink and blush roses are ideal for displaying in a large, floral jug with a cottage-garden design. It is important to choose vases which do not compete for attention through their size, colour or pattern – it is the pink roses which are important. When positioning the vase ensure curtains or wallpaper do not clash or overwhelm the flowers. Pink roses do not command attention in the same way as bright-yellow or sparkling-red ones. They have to be guarded from brash surrounds or their charm is lost.

When choosing roses for display, cut them early in the morning, when stems are full of moisture. Then, place them in deep buckets of cold, clean water for twenty-four hours. Take them out and remove the lower leaves and thorns. Re-cut the end of each stem at an angle and use a hammer to split the base for a few inches. Some flower arrangers like to remove all of the leaves to prevent them tainting the water. Ensure the water in the vase is topped up each day. As soon as a flower starts to fade, remove it; if left, it encourages decay to spread. Do not add fresh plants to the same water as they may also decay – it is better to wash the vase and add fresh water.

'Mullard Jubilee' is widely acclaimed in both England and North America. It develops large, moderately scented, deep rose-pink flowers, singly and in clusters. Plants are bushy and the flowers are borne amid dark-green, semi-glossy leaves. The blooms are resistant to damage from rain.

RIGHT 'Savoy Hotel' has large, lightly scented, light-pink blooms which develop deeper tones and therefore create an excitingly attractive display. Bushes grow about 90cm (3ft) high and develop dark-green leaves.

ABOVE 'Silver Jubilee' was introduced in 1978 and has been increasing in popularity ever since. Its large, shapely, peach-pink and rosy-salmon blooms have a sumptuous richness set off by the dense, dark, glossy foliage. They are borne on short stems and create a magnificent bedding variety, about 1m (3½ft) high. It is resistant to diseases and is on all counts an excellent garden rose.

OTHER PINK AND BLUSH HYBRID TEAS

✻ 'Abbeyfield Rose': Deep rosy-pink blooms freely borne amid bushy growth on bushes 60cm (2ft) tall. It is grown in beds in gardens and especially prized where space is scarce. It is also ideal for cutting and displaying indoors.

✻ 'Congratulations': Medium-sized, slightly scented, rose-pink blooms borne on lanky bushes up to 1.5m (5ft) high. With age, the blooms fade slightly.

✻ 'Dr McAlpine': Medium-sized, deep-pink blooms borne in clusters amid spreading, bushy growth. Bushes grow only 45cm (18in) tall.

✻ 'Heidi Jayne': Large, fragrant, deep-pink blooms and upright growth on plants 90cm (3ft) tall.

✻ 'Lady Sylvia': Introduced in 1927, this rose is still popular. It develops large, classically shaped, scented, pale-pink blooms in clusters amid upright growth on bushes which growo about 90cm (3ft) high.

✻ 'Madame Butterfly': Medium-sized, very fragrant, pale-pink blooms with yellow at their base.

✻ 'Marijke Koopman': Large, rich deep-pink blooms borne amid upright growth on plants more than 1m (3½ft) tall.

✻ 'My Choice': Large, very fragrant pink blooms with a light-yellow reverse. Growth is attractive and bushy and plants grow 75cm (2½ft) high.

✻ 'Ophelia': This is a long-established rose, introduced in 1912 and still grown by those who like to have a piece of rose history in their garden. Medium to large, very fragrant, pale-pink blooms with yellow at the base. Bushes have upright growth and grow to about 90cm (3ft) high.

✻ 'Queen Charlotte': Large, lightly scented, light reddish-salmon blooms on plants with upright growth to about 90cm (3ft) high.

✻ 'Royal Highness': This variety is well known in North America, where it has been highly acclaimed. The large, fragrant blooms are borne on bushes 1m (3½ft) high.

✻ 'Shot Silk': Large, well-scented, rosy salmon-pink blooms with a yellow base. Plants are bushy and usually grow about 50cm (20in) high.

✻ 'Susan Hampshire': Large, moderately scented, bright rose-pink blooms on plants with upright growth and about 75cm (2½ft) tall.

RIGHT 'Wendy Cussons' is well known as a rose for planting in gardens and has won many awards. The large, very fragrant, cherry-red to deep-pink blooms are borne amid bushy growth and on plants about 90cm (3ft) high. Some growers claim that its strong colour creates difficulties in finding companions. If this is a problem it can also be planted about 1.2m (4ft) from a white wall.

CRIMSON, SCARLET AND VERMILION HYBRID TEAS

These are dramatic, colour-saturated hues, ideal for creating spectacular displays of colour in rose gardens throughout the rose season. Occasionally, these colours are so deep that at twilight they appear to be black. In bright sunlight they are eye-catching and dominant.

MIXING AND MATCHING

When used in large, dramatic displays of colour, crimson, scarlet and vermilion flowers soon overpower and subdue lighter-coloured flowers close to them. For this reason, complete beds of these colours are often planted, so that the display is a dramatic colour feature on its own. Colour-wheels, in which representative and significant colours throughout the spectrum are arranged in order, are sometimes used to indicate both complementary and harmonizing colours. The complementary colour for red is green, the harmonizing ones (sharing some of the same pigments) are orange and violet. But acting on this information is not always straightforward. For example, a mid-green background to dark-red roses creates a three-dimensional effect, making the blooms appear to stand out, while harmonizing ones can, if the colours are too similar, create confusion to the eye. However, there are a few combinations of roses and other plants which make superb displays, such as:
• Plant *Pyrethrum aureum* 'Golden Moss' around the edge of a border of dominantly red roses. In late spring, after all risk of frost has gone, plant the

pyrethrum about 15cm (6in) apart. It grows about 10cm (4in) high and has golden-green, moss-like leaves and small, white flowers. If the rose bushes are planted more than 90cm (3ft) from the edge of the border, plant the edging in two staggered rows about 20cm (8in) apart so that a wider ruff is created.
• For a startling combination – best seen from a distance – plant a bed of red roses with a yellow-flowered yarrow between them. Select a yarrow which flowers at the same height as the roses. This type of companion planting is frequently seen in Germany, where yellow-flowered forms of the popular day lilies (*Hemerocallis*) are also used.
• Perennial, feathery grasses look superb when planted between red roses. Select roses with light-red flowers and use a grass such as Gardener's Gaiters (*Phalaris arundinacea* 'Picta') which grows about 60cm (2ft) high and develops long, narrow, upright then arching leaves variegated bright green and cream. This design looks good on a small scale and with the grass positioned both between and behind the roses.

TOP 'Ruby Wedding' develops medium-sized, slightly fragrant, ruby-red blooms on bushes with a branching nature, about 75cm (2½ft) high. It is an ideal Hybrid Tea rose for small gardens, as well as for cutting and displaying indoors.

ABOVE 'Alexander' is widely acclaimed and develops medium-sized, slightly fragrant, cherry-red blooms. Often, the petals have scalloped edges. Bushes are tall and vigorous and up to 1.5m (5ft) high. Indeed, it is tall enough to create a large hedge. The blooms on long stalks are ideal for cutting and displaying indoors.

LEFT 'Deep Secret' has large, very fragrant, richly coloured, deep-crimson blooms. Indeed, it is claimed to be the darkest of all red roses. Flowers are borne in small trusses rather than singly. Bushes are vigorous and upright, to about 90cm (3ft) tall.

'Madame Louis Laperrière' has a bushy habit, with medium-sized, scented, deep-crimson blooms borne on plants about 60cm (2ft) high. When young, the small leaves are reddish. It starts to flower early in the rose year and continues well into autumn.

'Loving Memory' has large, lightly scented, dark-red blooms borne amid upright growth on bushes often more than 90cm (3½ ft) high.

'National Trust' has medium-sized, bright-red blooms on erect bushes about 60cm (2ft) high. Its moderate stature, free-flowering nature and neat growth make it ideal for planting in rose beds in gardens. The foliage, when young, is coppery-red, which contributes to making it a spectacular rose.

OTHER CRIMSON, SCARLET AND VERMILION ROSES TO CONSIDER

* 'Alec's Red': Large and globular, very fragrant, cherry-red blooms borne on bushy plants about 90m (3ft) high.

* 'Barkarole': Some rose experts predict that this scented, deep-red rose (introduced in 1989) could become very popular. It has a classical appearance, a satiny sheen to the petals. Bushes grow about 90cm (3ft) high.

* 'Duke of Windsor': This scented, rosy-vermilion rose was introduced in 1968 and since then has been widely grown for its luminous quality. Bushes grow about 75cm (2½ft) tall.

* 'Ena Harkness': Large, very fragrant, crimson-scarlet blooms borne amid moderately vigorous, branching growth on plants 75cm (2½ft) tall.

* 'Ernest H. Morse': One of the finest red roses, popular and widely acclaimed. The large, fragrant, crimson blooms are borne prolifically throughout the rose season. It is ideal for planting in rose beds, growing for exhibition and cutting to decorate rooms indoors. Bushes grow 75cm (2½ft) high.

* 'Fragrant Cloud': One of the best-known red roses within the last thirty years. It has large, very fragrant, dusky-scarlet blooms borne amid vigorous, upright growth on bushes 75cm (2½ft) high. It is ideal for growing in beds, for exhibition and to cut for room decoration.

* 'Ingrid Bergman': Large, dark-red blooms and dark, leathery leaves. Bushes have an upright stance and grow about 82cm (32in) high.

* 'Josephine Bruce': Large, superbly fragrant, blackish-crimson blooms borne on bushes about 75cm (2½ft) tall.

* 'Malcolm Sargent': Introduced in 1988, it is expected to become one of the top red roses; ideal for growing in beds and the long stems assure it a place with flower arrangers. The shining-crimson blooms are lightly scented and borne on bushes 90cm (3ft) high.

* 'Roxburghe Rose': Medium-sized, lightly scented vermilion blooms borne in wide sprays and on plants about 75cm (2½ft) high.

* 'Super Star': This rose has been acclaimed by several generations and it still never fails to gain attention. The large, moderately scented vermilion flowers are borne on bushes about 90cm (3ft) high.

LEFT 'Red Devil', also known as 'Coeur d'Amour', is a superb rose, with large, fragrant, scarlet blooms with a pale-scarlet reverse. It is widely grown in beds, as well as for exhibiting and cutting to display indoors. The bushes, about 1m (3½ft) tall, are vigorous, upright and bushy. Unfortunately, it is not tolerant of wet weather and the blooms often become marked.

ABOVE 'Painted Moon' has flowers which are all colours to all eyes. They are a combination of crimson, pink and light yellow and borne in wide sprays amid bushy growth.

BELOW 'Velvet Fragrance' has large, fragrant, dark velvet-crimson blooms and upright growth which creates a bush about 1m (3½ft) high. Claims are made that it is the darkest and most fragrant of all red roses, and since its introduction in 1988 it has certainly gained in popularity. It is ideal for growing in borders as well as to cut for indoor display. The blooms can withstand inclement weather and are also resistant to diseases.

'Precious Platinum', also known as 'Red Star', was introduced in 1974 and has been widely planted in beds ever since. Its large, fragrant, bright-crimson blooms are borne freely in clusters. Bushes grow about 75cm (2½ft) high and reveal a vigorous, branching nature. It is ideal in gardens as the blooms have a good degree of resistance to diseases. But attention should be given to regular inspection of bushes for early signs of mildew.

ROSES AND LOVE

Red roses have a special association with love and passion and have assumed a romantic role unequalled by any other flower. The gift of a single red rose has been known to heal many a lovers' tiff, while the presentation of a dozen, long-stemmed blooms can restore a jaded marriage. When silent messages of love were passed between lovers in the language of flowers, roses were frequently chosen as romantic messengers. Different roses had different meanings and here are a few of them:
Burgundy rose: *Simplicity and beauty*.
Cabbage rose: *Ambassador of love*.
Red rosebud: *Pure and lovely*.
Single rose: *Simplicity*.
White and red roses together: *Unity/warmth of heart*.

White rose: *I am worthy of you/silence*.
White rose full of buds: *Secrecy*.
White rosebud: *Too young to love/girlhood*.
Withered white rose: *Transient impressions*.
Yellow rose: *Infidelity/jealousy*.

'Royal William' has proved to be a reliable and free-flowering rose since its introduction in 1987. It has medium-sized, fragrant, deep-red blooms borne amid vigorous, upright growth on bushes 1m (3½ft) tall. It is sturdy and performs well in both dry and wet seasons.

LILAC, BI-COLOURED AND STRIPED HYBRID TEAS

This group contains some of the most unusually coloured Hybrid Tea roses. They range from 'blue' roses to those known as bi-coloured (two distinct colours) and ones with distinctive stripes.

Bi-coloured roses have never become popular, striped ones even less, and yet they have originality and distinction which endears them to many gardeners in search of something different and unusual. Children often find them appealing and this can lead them on to a greater interest in roses. It is difficult to mix and match these unusual roses with others and they are best planted on their own or in a small group. They are exciting and interesting roses to have in a garden and their range is quite wide – some of these are described below – and each year further ones are added.

STRIPED ROSES

These are even more difficult than bi-coloured roses to associate with other roses. They immediately capture all the attention and do not enhance their bedding companions. If a bush of a striped variety is positioned near a patio or path edge it will introduce a talking point which seldom fails to divide the rose experts into two groups – those with traditional views and others who are more adventurous and experimental.

The best-known striped Hybrid Tea is 'Harry Wheatcroft', a sport of the bi-coloured 'Piccadilly', introduced in 1972. The large, pointed, slightly fragrant blooms are scarlet and attractively striped yellow.

The flowers are freely borne on compact bushes about 75cm (2½ ft) high, with glossy, dark-green leaves.

LEFT 'Blue Parfum' was introduced in 1978 in pursuit of the elusive blue rose. It has large, strongly scented, shapely, mauve-pink blooms on bushes about 75cm (2½ ft) tall. The blooms are larger than those of 'Blue Moon'.

'Blue Moon' is considered by rose experts to be the best 'blue' rose. It was introduced in 1964 and still remains an excellent rose, with lemon-scented, well-formed, lilac-mauve blooms borne on upright but branching bushes 90cm (3ft) high. It is prized by arrangers and often considered to be better when cut and displayed indoors.

OTHER BI-COLOURED ROSES

* 'Gay Gordons': Medium-sized, slightly fragrant blooms coloured orange-yellow and red. Bushes are vigorous and bushy, and 60–90cm (2–3ft) high.

* 'Kronenbourg': Also known as 'Flaming Peace', it has large, fragrant, crimson petals with an old-gold reverse. Bushes grow 1.2m (4ft) high.

* 'My Choice': Large, fragrant blooms with pink petals and a pale-yellow reverse. Bushes grow about 75cm (2½ ft) high.

* 'Rose Gaujard': Highly acclaimed, with large, slightly fragrant blooms, rose-red with a silvery reverse. Bushes grow 1m (3½ ft) high.

* 'Tenerife': A demure bi-colour with large, very fragrant, deep coral-salmon petals and a peach reverse. Bushes grow 75cm (2½ ft) high.

RIGHT 'Champion' has moderately scented, primrose-yellow flowers flushed pink. Its parents, 'Grandpa Dickson' and 'Whisky Mac', are well known and widely grown.

IN SEARCH OF BLUE ROSES

This is a quest rose-breeders have pursued for many decades. The best 'blue' variety so far produced is 'Blue Moon', introduced in 1964 from a cross between an unnamed seedling and 'Sterling Silver', which was a 1957 introduction with silvery-lilac blooms, a cross between an unnamed seedling and the world-famous 'Peace'. This is basically a yellow variety, with 'Joanna Hill' (yellow), 'Charles P. Kilham' (reddish-orange), 'Margaret McGredy' (orange-scarlet to crimson) and *Rosa foetida* (the Persian yellow

rose) in its parentage. With such a medley of genes – and no blue parent – it is remarkable that 'Blue Moon' has such a 'blue' nature. Genetically, it is probable that no true blue rose will ever be raised. This is because the blue pigment known as delphinidin is not present in the rose family, but hope is the central motivation when breeding roses.

'Big Purple' is an eye-catching Hybrid Tea rose, with beetroot-purple blooms borne on upright, leggy bushes about 90cm (3ft) high. The flowers are moderately scented and borne amid dark-green leaves. Sometimes this variety is known as 'Stephens' Big Purple'.

'Piccadilly' is one of the best and most popular of bi-coloured roses. The prime colour is scarlet, with pale-yellow reverses. The medium-sized, slightly fragrant blooms which are freely produced make it a superb rose for planting in beds in gardens.

SCENTED HYBRID TEAS

Scented roses are rather like the cream on an already beautiful cake; fragrance, rich or sweet, adds a special, mysterious quality to roses which is much sought after and brings great delight. Many Hybrid Tea roses are scented to some degree; a few of those admired for their combination of fragrance and flower colour are shown here. Whereas colour can be appreciated from a distance, especially when large beds are planted with the same variety, fragrance is more elusive. The bushes need to be planted in a warm, sheltered area and particularly at the side of a path for their scent to be appreciated. There is little point in growing scented roses if they are positioned at the back of a border.

Scented bush roses can be concentrated in one area, perhaps as part of a larger feature – round a garden seat or where arches and trellises are formed over paths. Keep the garden paths wide, so that it is possible to walk along them side-by-side with a partner. When admiring plants it is so much pleasanter to stroll beside a fellow plant admirer than to string along in an unsociable follow-my-leader style. Scented flowers also have special appeal to people who are partially sighted, so if there is someone in the household with poor or little sight, make the path with wide paving slabs and make a gravel strip at each side. When using the path, the person with limited vision will then be warned by the sound of treading on gravel and will be less likely to walk into thorny bushes.

LEFT 'My Choice' has large, very fragrant, pink flowers with a light-yellow reverse to the petals. Apart from its strong scent, it has several other virtues, including rich flower colour, resistance to disease and strong growth. It has bushy growth and reaches about 75cm (2½ft) high.

LEFT 'Ophelia' was introduced many decades ago and still brings beauty to gardens with its fragrant and delicate pale-pink flowers which are shaded yellow at their base. The classically shaped blooms are borne in large clusters on moderately vigorous, upright bushes which reach about 90cm (3ft) high. It is ideal for planting in beds in gardens, as well as displaying in floral decorations. Early flowers are at risk from the pest thrips and therefore spraying may be necessary.

'Barkarole' displays large, scented, deep-red blooms on bushes about 90cm (3ft) high and 75cm (2½ft) wide. The beautiful flowers are borne amid a mass of glossy leaves.

'The McCartney Rose' creates a mass of scented, large, deep-pink flowers on vigorous bushes which grow to about 1m (3½ft) high and 90cm (3ft) wide.

OTHER SCENTED HYBRID TEAS

* ✳ 'Blue Parfum': Mauve-pink (page 46)
* ✳ 'Deep Secret': Deep crimson (page 42)
* ✳ 'Dr McAlpine': Deep pink (page 41)
* ✳ 'Duke of Windsor': Rosy-vermilion (page 44)
* ✳ 'Ernest H. Morse': Red (page 44)
* ✳ 'Heidi Jayne': Bright, deep pink (page 41)
* ✳ 'Just Joey': Coppery-orange (page 35)
* ✳ 'Mary Donaldson': Salmon pink (page 39)
* ✳ 'Papa Meilland': Blackish crimson (page 44)
* ✳ 'Paul Shirville': Soft salmon-pink (page 38)
* ✳ 'Pink Peace': Deep pink (page 39)
* ✳ 'Pot o' Gold': Yellow (page 32)
* ✳ 'Rosemary Harkness': Orange-yellow (page 36)
* ✳ 'Royal Highness': Flesh pink (page 41)
* ✳ 'Royal William': Deep red (page 45)
* ✳ 'Shot Silk': Rosy salmon-pink (page 41)
* ✳ 'Valencia': Light amber-yellow (page 33)
* ✳ 'Wendy Cussons': Red to deep pink (page 41)
* ✳ 'Whisky Mac': Golden-apricot (page 37)

ABOVE 'Alec's Red' has two superb roses in its parentage: 'Fragrant Cloud' is famous for its scented, dusky-scarlet flowers, while 'Dame de Coeur' has large, cherry-red blooms. The result is large, globular, richly fragrant, cherry-red flowers borne on bushy plants about 90cm (3ft) high. It is ideal for growing in beds in gardens, exhibiting and cutting to display indoors.

'Double Delight' is an American rose, introduced in 1977 and widely grown ever since. It combines blush-pink petals, edged and flushed carmine, with a rich fragrance. The blooms are borne over a long period and last for a long time. The proportion of the two colours on the petals is variable, but they always look superb. The vigorous bushes branch unevenly and grow about 90cm (3ft) high.

FLORIBUNDA ROSES

Floribundas do not have the formal elegant blooms of the Hybrid Tea roses but they have quantities of flowers that bring colour to the garden over a long season. They are now properly known as Cluster-flowered roses and their relaxed, informal style enables them to blend well into mixed borders surrounded by shrubs and other border plants. They are very adaptable and can be used in many ways. They are particularly effective planted beside a garage drive or as a flowering screen between the front garden and the road.

Floribundas flower almost continually throughout the summer and autumn. When planning their positions in gardens, do not just use them with other roses; try mixing and matching them with herbaceous perennials, dwarf box hedges or with a backing of larger hedges and shrubs. Throughout this section about Floribundas, many ideas about using roses are suggested. And there is always the possibility of using some of them to form flowering hedges (*see pages 78 and 79*).

The range of white and cream floribunda roses is surprisingly limited, yet for creating a look of freshness and serenity a white floribunda has few rivals. The massed heads of white flowers are a lovely sight on a summer's day.

MIXING AND MATCHING

The cool, refreshing style of white Floribundas is more relaxed than white-flowered Hybrid Teas, because of their cluster-flowered nature. They should not be placed among dominantly coloured flowers, or those with a large and strong outline. Green, silver and light pink are some combinations to consider:

• Surround a rose bed with a low hedge of the small-leaved, glossy and dark-green, evergreen box (*Buxus sempervirens* 'Suffruticosa'). It can be clipped to form a hedge 38–45cm (15–18in) high.

• For an informal edging, plant the lamb's tongue (*Stachys byzantina*, also known as *S. olympica* and *S. lanata*). This has large leaves covered with silvery-white hairs and forms irregular mounds 30–38cm (12–15in) high. Spikes of purple-blue flowers appear in mid-summer and if they confuse your eye and dominate the rose, cut them off to leave the attractive leaves.

• White or pale-pink old-fashioned pinks (*Dianthus*) could also be used as an edging, especially for low-growing white Floribundas.

• The stately and slow-growing yew (*Taxus baccata*) creates an ideal background for pure white floribundas. The yew needs a strong contrast and will not show up cream-coloured flowers as well as pure white ones.

RIGHT 'Grüss an Aachen' creates a feast of blush-pink to creamy-white flowers amid upright growth. The bushes grow about 45cm (1.5ft) high and wide. It is moderately scented and develops dark, leathery leaves. In its parentage it has the well-known white-flowered Hybrid Perpetual 'Frau Karl Druschki', which is also known as 'Snow Queen' and 'White American Beauty'.

'Iceberg', introduced in 1958 from a cross between 'Robin Hood' and 'Virgo', is outstanding for its showy clusters of white flowers, which appear continuously throughout summer and often well into winter. During very hot weather the flowers sometimes become slightly pink. The individual flowers are medium to large and borne on bushes about 75cm (2½ ft) high. In country areas, rabbits are likely to nibble at the shiny, light-green leaves.

ABOVE 'Yvonne Rabier', introduced in 1910 from a cross between *R. wichuraiana* and a white polyantha, bears clusters of milk-white, small blooms on bushy but compact plants about 45cm (1½ ft) high. The fragrant flowers are freely borne in medium-sized trusses. The bush benefits from being only lightly pruned.

BELOW 'Many Happy Returns' is sometimes described as a Floribunda, other times as a Cluster-flowered shrub. Its flower colour is also variably described, from blush-white to blush-pink and light blush. It flowers early in the rose season and in autumn the flowers are followed by orange-red hips.

'Margaret Merril', introduced in 1977, is strong competition for 'Iceberg'. Its large, richly scented, dainty, high-centred blooms are only blush-white but they have a better scent. The flowers are especially prized for their satin sheen, a quality not often found in modern roses. The bushy, upright growth is borne on plants about 82cm (32in) high.

RIGHT 'Golden Years', introduced in 1990, develops large, richly golden-yellow flowers on bushes 60–75cm (2–2½ ft) high. It is the progeny of the yellow-flowered 'Sunblest' and the amber-yellow 'Amber Queen'.

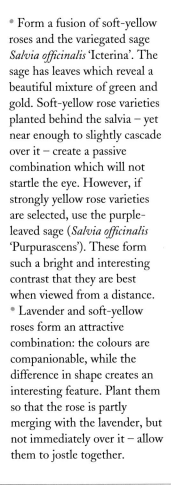

YELLOW FLORIBUNDA ROSES

These are popular and guaranteed to introduce brightness and vitality into borders and beds during a major part of summer.

There are many varieties to choose from, in a range of yellows from bright and radiant to those with a primrose hue. Most retain their colour in strong sunlight, but varieties like 'Sunsilk' and 'Arthur Bell' are likely to fade – though not dramatically.

MIXING AND MATCHING

Strongly coloured yellow roses create opportunities to mix other strong colours with them, as well as large but paler flowers. Combinations to consider include:
• The bright-yellow 'Allgold' combines with the mid- and late-summer flowering *Clematis* 'Countess of Lovelace'. Allow this deep lavender-coloured, large-flowered hybrid to scramble through the rose.
• A hedge formed of a bright-yellow rose, such as 'Mountbatten', looks superb when backed by tall, rich-blue delphiniums. Leave a space of about 1.2m (4ft) between the hedge and delphiniums, so that the plants can be looked after.
• The silver leaves of lamb's tongue (*Stachys byzantina*, but better known as *S. olympica* and *S. lanata*) harmonize with light, soft yellows. Strong yellows create too much impact and 'kill' the beauty of the silver-haired leaves.

ABOVE 'Arthur Bell' develops large, golden-yellow flowers singly and in clusters on vigorous and upright bushes, about 82cm (32in) high. The colour fades slightly with age and becomes pale cream. It is a variety which has been acclaimed for its rich scent and ability to flower from early to late in the rose year. Also, it is resistant to black spot and mildew.

• Form a fusion of soft-yellow roses and the variegated sage *Salvia officinalis* 'Icterina'. The sage has leaves which reveal a beautiful mixture of green and gold. Soft-yellow rose varieties planted behind the salvia – yet near enough to slightly cascade over it – create a passive combination which will not startle the eye. However, if strongly yellow rose varieties are selected, use the purple-leaved sage (*Salvia officinalis* 'Purpurascens'). These form such a bright and interesting contrast that they are best when viewed from a distance.
• Lavender and soft-yellow roses form an attractive combination: the colours are companionable, while the difference in shape creates an interesting feature. Plant them so that the rose is partly merging with the lavender, but not immediately over it – allow them to jostle together.

ABOVE 'Amber Queen', also known as 'Prinz Eugen' and 'Harroony', develops fragrant, medium-sized, amber-yellow flowers in large clusters. When young the leaves are reddish, but slowly become dark green. They are borne on bushy, moderately vigorous plants about 50cm (20in) high. This variety was introduced in 1984 and has gained many awards for its colour, stature and freely flowering habit. Its low and compact nature makes it ideal for small gardens.

OTHER YELLOW FLORIBUNDAS

❋ 'Burma Star': Large, light-amber flowers on upright bushes, 1.2m (4ft) high.

❋ 'Golden Wedding': Large, bright-yellow flowers on bushes 82cm (32in) high.

❋ 'Honeymoon': Medium-sized and rosette-shaped, canary-yellow flowers on bushes 90cm (3ft) high.

❋ 'Mr JCB': Sulphur-yellow flowers with a hint of red on reverses. Bushes 75cm (2½ ft) high.

❋ 'Princess Alice': Large clusters of bright-yellow flowers on bushes up to 1m (3½ ft) high.

❋ 'Princess Michael of Kent': Large, well-shaped, canary-yellow flowers and shiny leaves. Bushes grow about 75cm (2½ ft) high.

❋ 'Sunsilk': Large, lemon-yellow flowers borne on bushes 82cm (32in) high. The double flowers are borne in large clusters and upright growth.

'Korresia', beautifully and also aptly known as 'Sunsprite', has fragrant, bright-yellow flowers with wavy petals. It was introduced in 1974, has gained in popularity ever since and now rivals 'Allgold' as the perfect yellow-flowered Floribunda rose. It is ideal for planting in flower-beds in gardens as well as for cutting to decorate rooms indoors. The flowers are borne on dense, moderately vigorous bushes about 75cm (2½ ft) tall.

'Bright Smile', also known as 'Dicdance', was introduced in 1980. The bright-yellow flowers are rather sparsely packed with petals, but as the blooms are plentifully borne in clusters this is not a serious problem, although to some eyes it is an initial upset. Nevertheless, it is widely acclaimed and creates an attractive display, with the bushes about 45cm (1½ ft) tall.

'Mountbatten' is a vigorous and tall-growing Floribunda rose, about 1.2m (4ft) high. It has large, mimosa-yellow flowers borne in small clusters and has received many awards for its colour, ease of growing and resistance to diseases. However, it is not a rose which can be squeezed into a small space and to be seen to perfection requires a large bed.

APRICOT, COPPER AND ORANGE FLORIBUNDA ROSES

These colours bring a glowing warmth and a sense of well-being to gardens. While they do not have the dramatic colour impact of vivid reds and bright yellows, nor the discreet charm of light pinks and white they have attractive qualities. They are especially appealing in gardens in late summer and autumn to complement early autumnal colours.

They can also be used in beds of bold colour. They neither brighten dramatically when in strong sunlight, nor dull too much when seen in the waning light of evening.

BELOW 'Anne Harkness' straddles the dividing line between colours: some experts say apricot-yellow, others apricot. The flowers are medium-sized and borne in large clusters on strong, upright bushes about 1.2m (4ft) high. It is an excellent variety to provide colour during mid- and late summer, when it is most often needed. It is ideal for planting in beds, cutting for indoor decoration and to exhibit in shows.

LEFT 'Apricot Nectar' was introduced in 1965 and is still popular and widely recommended by rose experts. The large, moderately scented flowers are formed of pale-apricot petals which shade to gold at their base. They appear singly or in clusters. The foliage is medium green and glossy and borne on bushy plants about 60cm (2ft) high.

MIXING AND MATCHING

Mixing apricot, copper and orange with other plants is not easy, but off-white and dull silver can always be relied upon to create backgrounds and border edgings. As they do not command attention they are excellent foils for richer coloured flowers.

When robust and tall, apricot, copper and orange Floribunda roses can be planted in mixed borders, where they live happily with shrubs and herbaceous plants, as their relaxed colours do not compete. This is especially true in late summer and early autumn when the leaves of many deciduous shrubs start to assume rich colours.

Similarly coloured chrysanthemum and dahlia flowers are suitable bedfellows in late summer and until the frosts of autumn, but use them sparingly so that attention is focused on the roses. In fact, chrysanthemums and dahlias are even more compatible when some of their flowers have been picked for display in vases indoors.

'Avocet' develops clusters of medium-sized, pale-orange flowers edged in coppery-pink. It was introduced in 1981.

LEFT 'Southampton', with its slightly ruffled, apricot-orange and occasionally pink-flushed flowers, has become popular since its introduction in 1972. It is ideal in borders, as a cut flower for room decoration and as a hedge. Its growth is vigorous and upright, often to 1.2m (4ft), and it has won many international awards.

MIXED BORDERS

These are borders where herbaceous perennials, shrubs, bulbous plants and annuals are mixed together. Hybrid Teas do not normally happily co-habit in this way, but Floribundas are more adaptable to it, especially those that develop into large bushes.

Apricot-, copper- and orange-flowered varieties especially harmonize in these borders. Do not position them in rows, but rather arrange them at random with some near the back and others in the middle.

These colours introduce warmth into a border during mid-summer, with their hues imitated and followed by orange dahlias and chrysanthemums later in the summer.

Do not crowd other plants too closely around the roses as it intrudes on their form and restricts the flow or air around and between stems, encouraging the presence of pests and diseases. Removing dead flowers helps to improve the circulation of air and to reduce the incidence of disease.

'Glenfiddich', a Floribunda, creates a vivid display of amber-yellow, moderately-scented flowers amid glossy, dark green leaves. It has an upright stance, about 75cm (2½ft) high and 90cm (2ft) wide, and was introduced in 1976.

LEFT 'Playboy' develops clusters of medium-sized, orange-yellow flowers shaded scarlet. Growth is bushy, with dark, glossy-green leaves.

OTHER APRICOT, COPPER AND ORANGE FLORIBUNDAS

* 'Daylight': Medium-sized, buff-apricot flowers on bushes 90cm (3ft) high. Long flowering period.

* 'Fellowship': Flowers said to be a fusion of Spanish orange and glowing embers. Bushes grow to 90cm (3ft) high. Ideal for bedding and hedging.

* 'Harold Macmillan': Distinctive, Indian-orange flowers on bushes about 75cm (2½ft) high.

* 'Julie Cussons': Brilliant orange-salmon flowers on bushes 90cm (3ft) high. Superb fragrance.

* 'Pensioner's Voice': Bright orange-apricot flowers, with tints of pink and vermilion, on strong bushes which grow about 90cm (3ft) high.

* 'Woburn Abbey': Golden-orange flowers borne in large clusters on bushes 90cm (3ft) high.

RIGHT 'Paddy McGredy' is another pink Floribunda which has been in cultivation for several decades, having been introduced in 1962. It develops clusters of large, slightly fragrant, rose-carmine or deep rose-pink flowers amid glossy, dark-green leaves. The flower colour tends to fade when in hot sunshine. Bushes are branching, moderately vigorous and up to 45cm (1½ft) high.

'Mr. E. E. Greenwell', was raised in 1979 with 'Jove' and 'City of Leeds' in its parentage. It is a small, compact bush which grows to 60cm (2ft) and has coral-pink flowers and medium-green foliage.

PINK AND BLUSH FLORIBUNDAS

Pink is a gentle and reserved shade in the colour spectrum; neither as clinical as white nor as rich a colour as red. In fact, pink contains only a small proportion of red pigments. For this reason, it is easier to mix and match it with other plants in gardens than the fiery reds, which can be extremely dominant. Even within the pink range the colours vary widely, from blush to a rich pink only a few shades less than light red.

MIXING AND MATCHING

Pink Floribunda roses can be used to create many attractive combinations of plants in gardens. Here are a few of them to consider:

• Plant the low-growing, 45cm (1½ft) high, salmon-pink and slightly fragrant 'Tip Top' between drifts of the low-growing *Lavandula angustifolia* 'Munstead' and interplant with *Lilium regale*, which displays white, funnel-shaped flowers in loose clusters during mid-summer. An edging of the silver-leaved lamb's tongue (*Stachys byzantina*) completes the design. If you prefer Hybrid Tea roses, use 'Pascali' or 'Bonsoir' instead of 'Tip Top'.

• Choose a light-blush rose variety and plant a sea of light blue or white pansies (*Viola × wittrockiana*) around it. In addition, use an edging of the low-growing, blue-grey foliaged *Ruta graveolens* 'Jackman's Blue'.

• The cyclamen-pink flowers of 'Queen Elizabeth' look superb when planted with lavender and rosemary. Prune the rose severely, so that it grows about 1.5m (5ft) high, then plant groups of the 45–60cm (1½–2)ft high and deep purple *Lavandula* 'Hidcote' in front. Interplant them with mauve-flowered *Rosmarinus officinalis*. When the rosemary grows too large it can be cut down or replaced, but it can usually be kept quite low and bushy by repeatedly pinching out its growing tips when young.

• A combination of a late-flowering rose with warm, salmon-pink flowers and the 15cm (6in) high, early autumn to early-winter flowering *Gentiana sino-ornata* is superb. The gentian has brilliant-blue, 5cm (2in)-long, flowers with

RIGHT 'Dearest', introduced in 1960, has large, spicily fragrant, salmon-pink or light rosy-pink, camellia-like flowers borne in large clusters. Bushes are vigorous and branching and about 60cm (2ft) high. It is not as popular now as in earlier years, but still well worth planting in beds and for cutting to decorate rooms indoors. Unfortunately, it is susceptible to the diseases black spot and mildew.

deep-blue and greenish-yellow stripes. If you start with only a few gentians, they can be easily increased by pegging down their stems into moisture-retentive, friable soil.

• Some of the tall herbaceous artemisias create cool backgrounds for light to medium pinks. Choose rose varieties which grow about 60cm (2ft) high and plant a screen of the 45–60cm (1½–2ft) high *Artemisia gnaphalodes* behind it. Because the roses will be viewed with a downward angle, they will be seen as highlights of pink against the woolly, white leaves of the artemisia. During late summer and early autumn, the artemisia develops silver-white, brown-tipped flowers.

LEFT 'Champagne Cocktail' creates a spectacular display of flowers, a combination of pink and light yellow. These are borne on vigorous bushes, about 1m (3½ft) high. The flowers are only moderately scented.

'Radox Bouquet', introduced in 1981, has pure rose-pink flowers with a cottage-garden look, and for this reason, they are much prized by flower arrangers. It is equally at home in garden beds and merges well with shrubs in mixed borders. It also forms an attractive hedge. Bushes grow about 1m (3½ft) high.

OTHER PINK FLORIBUNDAS

✻ 'Anisley Dickson': Deep salmon-pink and lightly fragrant. Bushes grow 90cm (3ft) high.

✻ 'English Miss': Rosy-blush with deep-pink edges. Very fragrant, with bushes about 75cm (2½ft) high.

✻ 'Sea Pearl': Light pink with a peach-yellow reverse. Bushes grow 90cm (3ft) high.

✻ 'Sexy Rexy': Rose-pink, camellia-shaped and lightly scented. Bushes grow 72cm (28in) high.

✻ 'Shona': Coral-pink and slightly fragrant. Bushes grow about 75cm (2½ft) high.

✻ 'Valentine Heart': Soft-pink, frill-edged petals. Bushes grow 60cm (2ft) high.

✻ 'Wishing': Deep salmon-pink flowers with a Hybrid Tea shape. Bushes grow about 50cm (20in) high.

RED AND VERMILION FLORIBUNDAS

These are strong colours, dominant and immediately eye-catching. For this reason they can overwhelm more subtle and delicate colours around them. There is a wide range of Floribundas with red or vermilion flowers; they range from light reds, which are nearly pink, to vivid ones like the well-known 'Chorus' and 'Evelyn Fison'.

'Tornado' is a compact Floribunda with bright-red flowers and was raised by Kordes in 1973. It grows to about 75cm (2½ft) high.

MIXING AND MATCHING

Dominant reds are more difficult to mix and match than those with a softer and subdued nature. Here are a few planting arrangements to try:

• Use small groups of 'Evelyn Fison' (deep bright-red), 'Peer Gynt' (bright yellow with red flushes) and 'Whisky Mac' (amber-yellow) planted against a background of the North American evergreen shrub *Mahonia pinnata* and an underplanting of the lesser periwinkle (*Vinca minor*). The mahonia grows 2.4–3m (8–10ft) high and 2.4m (8ft) wide and has slightly fragrant, rich-yellow flowers during spring. While the mahonia creates early colour, later when its flowers have faded, the blooms of the rose will be highlighted against the mahonia's sea-green leaves.

'Intrigue' develops showy clusters of dark-red flowers amid bushy growth. Incidentally, this variety should not be confused with the reddish-purple variety of the same name, raised in North America in 1984.

ABOVE 'Lady Taylor' is sometimes classified as a low-growing Foribunda, at other times as a Patio Rose. Whatever the dispute over its grouping it is a superb rose with fragrant, vermilion flowers. Bushes are moderately vigorous with semi-glossy, medium-green leaves.

BELOW 'Invincible' creates a feast of bright crimson borne in large clusters on bushes 28cm (70in) high and amid glossy foliage. It is the progeny of 'Rubella' and the well-known 'National Trust'.

RIGHT 'Anne Cocker' is popular for its bright-vermilion flowers which are borne in neatly spaced, large clusters on vigorous and upright bushes, about 90cm (3ft) high. It is ideal for planting in garden beds, as well as for cutting to arrange indoors. Occasionally it is grown as an exhibition rose.

'Evelyn Fison', introduced in 1963 and also known as 'Irish Wonder', is a well-established and widely grown bright-red Floribunda, with large trusses of well-spaced flowers. Part of its success is the non-fading blooms and their resistance to damage from heavy rain storms. It is ideal when planted in beds in gardens, where it grows about 75cm (2½ ft) high.

- In a bed of strongly red Floribundas, plant pansies (*Viola × wittrockiana*) with predominantly yellow, blue and white colours. These summer-flowering pansies bloom from early summer to early autumn. Several strongly coloured varieties are available; avoid those with subdued tones or multi-coloured faces, as they will be unable to compete for attention with red roses.
- Light-grey stone walls form attractive backgrounds for strongly red roses. Grey-green walls are also suitable, but avoid green ones as they create optical illusions when red roses are planted in front of them. Some older-type Floribundas, such as 'Frensham', which forms a large shrub when not regularly pruned, can be allowed to sprawl against a well-weathered wall. Bush types are best planted several feet away from a wall; do not position them in the dry soil which often surrounds walls.
- Grow red roses with yellow ones to give a bold colour contrast, but use more yellow bushes than red ones, especially if strongly coloured ones are used. If equal numbers are planted, the red ones may appear to swamp the yellows.

BUTTONHOLES

The fashion for men to wear a rose in their buttonhole has all but gone except at weddings, and then the buttonhole is usually a festive creation of carnations. At one time, the wearing of a buttonhole by a man signalled to women his availability and willingness to respond to any amorous approach they might make.

So popular was the wearing of a buttonhole that at the beginning of the twentieth century metal tubes were made for fitting into jacket lapels. They could be filled with water to keep the flower fresh all day.

Buttonholes were fashionable in Europe, as well as in Britain, and no gentleman would consider being seen outside without one. Some men followed the fashion of wearing buttonholes with such dedication that they would not wear a rose of the same colour twice in one week.

ABOVE 'Fred Loads' has a vigorous, shrubby nature, with large clusters of coral-red flowers on strong, upright bushes. The plants often grow 1.8m (6ft) high.

'Glad Tidings' is a superb Floribunda, with clusters of dark-crimson blooms borne amid bushy growth. The bushes grow about 75cm (2½ft) high and the flowers have a moderate scent.

RED AND VERMILION FLORIBUNDAS

These dramatic and dominating colours are a popular choice with gardeners, a fact reflected in the range featured in rose catalogues. A glance through lists of Floribunda roses in catalogues and books confirms their continuing popularity. In some catalogues the subtleties of these colours are finely classified and graded from salmon-red to deep scarlet, with orange-scarlet, cerise-carmine, deep scarlet and scarlet-crimson between them. Whether these subtleties of shade are appreciated by all gardeners is doubtful, especially as up to six per cent of men suffer from some form of colour blindness. Some of them are unable to distinguish between red and green, especially when the light intensity is low. The existence of such a wide range of reds and associated colours indicates both the demand for them and the efforts of rose-breeders to satisfy that demand.

In fact, the popularity of these colours among rose-growers has remained constant. Lists of Floribundas in the 1950s show about a third of the recommendations were red and the proportion is the same today. There is no explanation for this traditional fondness for red roses but some gardeners believe it may be linked to their romantic associations.

HEALTHY RED ROSES

For many gardeners, a trouble-free rose which is resistant to diseases such as mildew and black spot is essential, especially when grown in damp and cold regions. Roses which have been correctly planted and later pruned properly and fed and watered regularly are less likely to become infected than those which are neglected, planted in poor soil and left to become a mass of tangled shoots and stems which prevent the entry of light and air.

'Memento' has an abundance of beautiful, slightly fragrant, salmon-red to cherry-pink flowers throughout the summer. They are resistant to damage from rain storms, as well as diseases. Plants are bushy, vigorous and upright, with dark-green leaves and about 75cm (2½ft) high. In a garden planted with several dark-red roses, its lighter colour is very welcome.

Wild roses and their near relatives often have a natural ability to coexist with diseases, especially when they are grown in their native areas. This ability is sometimes passed on to their progeny. However, when roses are especially bred for characteristics such as colour, shape and a long flowering period, some of the genetic characteristics which gave tolerance to diseases may be lost.

Several years ago it was accepted that the use of garden chemicals to combat both pests and diseases was the only way forward in the endless search for the 'perfect' rose. Today, this thinking has changed dramatically and most gardeners are thinking 'green'. More attention is being given to creating varieties with tolerance to diseases and thereby reducing the necessity to use chemicals, except as a last resort. Climbing and Shrub roses are invariably healthier than bush roses, but some Floribundas, such as 'The Times Rose', also have resistance to diseases and these roses are clearly identified where appropriate.

'Lilli Marlene' is a superb bedding rose as well as ideal for cutting to create attractive floral displays indoors. The velvety, deep-crimson flowers form a handsome combination with the coppery foliage and it has the virtue of being unaffected by rain storms and the often dulling strength of strong sunlight. Bushes are vigorous and about 75cm ($2^1/_2$ft) high.

ABOVE 'Trumpeter', introduced in 1978, has large, showy trusses of medium-sized, bright-vermilion flowers, but which are described by some rose experts as orange-red. Plants are bushy, leafy and about 50cm (20in) high.

RIGHT 'The Times Rose', introduced in 1982, has received many awards for its large, slightly fragrant dark-red flowers which are borne in large trusses on vigorous bushes about 60cm (2ft) high. The flowers open flat when mature and create a spectacular display when planted in beds. It has won the President's International Trophy of the British Royal National Rose Society, adding to its excellent reputation. Its health is usually good, as the plant and flowers are resistant to diseases.

ABOVE 'News' has beetroot-purple flowers with golden stamens borne on strong, bushy plants about 75cm (2½ft) tall. It was introduced in 1969 and has remained popular, its dramatic and unusually coloured flowers creating dominant splashes of colour. The leaves are dark and borne on upright stems.

LAVENDER, MAUVE AND PURPLE FLORIBUNDA ROSES

Although these colours are unusual for Floribundas and range is limited, they provide an opportunity for introducing something different into gardens. In addition to 'Lilac Charm', 'Lavender Pinocchio' and 'News' (*left*), there are a few other varieties to consider, such as:

• 'Purple Splendour': Introduced in 1976, it develops large flowers packed with clear, glowing-purple petals borne on erect stems and bushes up to 90cm (3ft) high.

• 'Shocking Blue': Introduced in 1974, it develops very fragrant, lilac-mauve flowers on plants with bushy growth and up to 75cm (2½ft) high. The flowers have a Hybrid Tea character and are popular with flower arrangers.

'Purple Tiger', raised in 1992, has deep purple flowers with white stripes and flecks and medium-green foliage. It is a fragrant, thornless bush that grows to about 75cm (2½ft) high.

HAND-PAINTED FLORIBUNDA ROSES

These delightful flowers are called hand-painted because they have a mixture of colours which look as if they have been applied by hand, colours which appear like crayoning over a slightly differently coloured base. Usually, there is a white eye at the base.

'Picasso', introduced in 1970, is thought to have been the first hand-painted rose. It has a mixture of genes from close relations such as 'Marlena' (bright crimson) and 'Evelyn Fison' (deep bright-red) and more distant ones like 'Orange Sweetheart' (orange-pink) and 'Frühlingsmorgen' (pink with a primrose centre). 'Picasso', the famous progeny of these, has carmine colouring which looks as if it has been crayoned on to the blush base.

Other hand-painted Floribunda varieties have followed, including 'Laughter Lines' (*above right*) and 'Sue Lawley'. Others include 'Matangi' (rich orange-red with a white eye and reverse, about 75cm/2¹⁄₂ ft high) and 'Regensberg' (pink patterned with white, 40cm/16in high).

All of these hand-painted varieties quickly capture attention and have a powerful charm, but they are not easy to mix with other varieties and are best either planted on their own or put in small groups, or among shrubs in a mixed border. They are particularly attractive when planted near a patio.

RIGHT 'Oranges and Lemons' develops clusters of orange-yellow flowers, striped and partly coloured scarlet. The coppery young foliage is also attractive.

LEFT 'Laughter Lines', widely known as a hand-painted variety, has flowers which are a kaleidoscope of colour, sometimes described as red, gold and white on a rosy-pink base. They are medium-sized flowers and borne on bushy plants nearly 75cm (2¹⁄₂ ft) high. The flowers have little scent, but this is more than compensated for by the unusual and brightly coloured flowers.

UNUSUAL SHADES

Rose experts are always searching for unusual shades or mixtures of colours in roses. A range of these includes:
- 'Brownie': Shades of tan flowers edged with pink.
- 'Edith Holden': Also known as 'The Edwardian Lady', it has russet-brown flowers with gold tints.
- 'Greensleeves': (*right*).
- 'Jocelyn': Dull mahogany, ageing to purple-brown flowers.
- 'Masquerade': A bright mixture of colours, yellow buds changing to pink then to red and the prolific flowers, a medley of all three colours at the same time. It is often grown as a multi-coloured hedge, about 1.2m (4ft) high, or mixed with shrubs in borders. It is too vibrant to be mixed with other roses.

'Greensleeves' is a rose with a difference, the pinkish-green buds opening to chartreuse-green blooms. The medium to large flowers are borne in loose clusters on leggy plants about 90cm (3ft) high. It is prized by flower arrangers seeking something unusual, but as a garden plant it has drawbacks, being susceptible to black spot and forming leggy, unattractive plants.

SCENTED FLORIBUNDAS

Fragrant Floribundas are a sheer delight in all gardens and are equally superb in beds on their own or arranged with other plants in mixed borders. Some can be planted to form hedges to separate one part of a garden from another, and the flowers are also excellent for cutting and displaying indoors in flower arrangements.

To ensure the rose's fragrance is enjoyed and is not diminished by strong winds, choose a wind-sheltered position and plant several bushes together. Positioning them close to a path makes them readily accessible.

APPRECIATING SCENT

Everyone, except those unfortunates who suffer from anosmia (loss of the sense of smell) is able to enjoy the wonderful scents of the garden. Interestingly, women have a keener sense of smell than men, but this sense deteriorates when they are pregnant. Nose colds and sinus problems clearly hinder the appreciation of smell. Age is no advantage in this matter as young people are better able to detect fragrances than the elderly. Perhaps surprisingly, indoor workers are often much better at identifying odours than people who work outdoors.

ABOVE 'City of London', introduced in 1988, has been widely praised for its sweet, rich fragrance, as well as the deep, mother-of-pearl flowers which pale towards their edges. When pruned lightly it reaches about 1.5m (5ft) high, but if severely cut it can be restrained to 90cm (3ft). The flowers are evenly spaced in their clusters.

'Harry Edland' reveals beautiful lilac-pink flowers and a rich fragrance. Bushes are branching and about 90cm (3ft) high. Its fragrance and rich colouring is not too surprising when its parentage is revealed – the Floribunda 'Lilac Charm' (light lilac and scented) and the Hybrid Tea 'Sterling Silver', with silvery-lilac, fragrant flowers. There are also 'Blue Moon' and 'Africa Star' in its pedigree.

ABOVE 'Southampton' develops clusters of large, apricot flowers with red flushes. They are well scented and appear on bushes with upright growth, to about 90cm (3½ ft) high.

'Scented Air' has, as its name suggests, richly scented, flowers. The deep salmon-pink blooms are large and shapely and borne in big, showy clusters on vigorous, upright bushes about 90cm (3ft) high. It is ideal for planting in beds in gardens, where it is appreciated more for its fragrance than its colour. It has won many awards and has good resistance to the onslaught of diseases.

OTHER SCENTED FLORIBUNDAS

In addition to the scented floribunda roses illustrated on these pages there are many others, including:

• 'Amber Queen': Amber-yellow flowers borne in large clusters (*page 52*).

• 'Apricot Nectar': Apricot-yellow shading to apricot flowers and in large clusters (*page 54*).

• 'Arthur Bell': Large, golden-yellow flowers becoming pale cream with age (*page 52*).

• 'Beauty Queen': Medium-pink flowers in large clusters on vigorous, upright bushes about 75cm (2¹/₂ ft) high.

• 'Burma Star': Large and light-amber flowers (*page 52*).

• 'Daylight': Unfading buff-apricot blooms on vigorous, bushy plants about 90cm (3ft) high. The young foliage is reddish, turning green with age.

LEFT
'Sheila's Perfume' is famed for its medium to large, strongly fragrant, yellow and red flowers with tight, high centres, which have the shape of Hybrid Tea blooms. Bushes are vigorous and grow to about 75cm (2½ft) high. It is ideal for growing in garden beds and to cut for displaying in flower arrangements indoors. For some rose-growers its lack of petals is a disadvantage, for others a delight. Plants have some resistance to diseases.

'Iced Ginger', introduced in 1971, is worth growing for its combination of scent and buff to coppery-pink, Hybrid Tea-shaped, flowers packed with many petals. The bushes are vigorous and upright, to 90cm (3ft) high. It can look sparse and leggy, but the flowers are in great demand by flower arrangers. Often it is grown as a hedge.

• 'Dearest': Medium-sized, rosy-pink flowers borne in large clusters on spreading bushes about 60cm (2ft) high.

• 'Dusky Maiden': Large, crimson flowers with deeper shadings and attractive golden anthers. Bushes grow about 75cm (2¹/₂ ft) high.

• 'Elizabeth of Glamis': Light, orange-salmon flowers borne on upright bushes about 75cm (2¹/₂ ft) high.

• 'English Miss': Ivory-blue flowers with deep-pink edges to the petals (page 57).

• 'Escapade': Rosy-violet flowers with white centres borne in large clusters on bushes with a shrubby habit and slightly more than 75cm (2¹/₂ ft) high.

• 'Fragrant Delight': Shapely, orange-salmon flowers borne in large, open clusters on

bushes with a vigorous, spreading habit up to 1m (3¹/₂ ft) high.

• 'Geranium Red': Large, full-petalled, sweetly scented, flat, dusky-red flowers tinged purple with age. Bushes grow about 75cm (2¹/₂ ft) high.

• 'Korresia': Bright-yellow, wavy-edged petals to the blooms make this rose much in demand, especially by flower arrangers (*page 53*).

• 'Margaret Merril': Large, blue-white and high-centred flowers with a satin sheen.

• 'Mountbatten': Tall, shrub-like Floribunda with large, mimosa-yellow, cup-shaped flowers. Bushes grow about 1.2m (4ft) high.

• 'Radox Bouquet': Pure rose-pink flowers, ideal in beds and flower arrangements. The blooms of this highly scented rose are often quartered and the bushes grow about 90cm (3ft) high and 60cm (2ft) wide (*page 57*).

• 'Shocking Blue': Lilac-mauve and greatly prized by flower arrangers (*page 62*).

• 'Valentine Heart': Soft-pink, semi-double flowers with frilled edges (*page 57*).

STANDARD ROSES

These are the sentries of the rose world; with their upright stance they tower above their bush companions, creating height and focal points either within a bed of bush roses or as single specimens in a lawn. There are several types of standard roses and many varieties:

• Standard roses are budded on to stocks 1m (39in) above the ground and eventually form heads 1.5–1.8m (5–6ft) high. Hybrid Tea varieties to choose from include: 'Dawn Chorus' (deep orange), 'Just Joey' (copper-orange), 'Loving Memory' (dark red), 'Paul Shirville' (soft salmon-pink), 'Peace' (yellow flushed pink), 'Royal William' (deep red), 'Ruby Wedding' (ruby red), 'Silver Wedding' (creamy-white), 'Simba' (clear yellow), 'Tequila Sunrise' (yellow, edged scarlet), 'Troika' (reddish-orange with yellow and pink) and 'Valencia' (amber-yellow).

• Floribunda varieties used for standard roses include: 'Amber Queen' (amber-yellow), 'Anna Livia' (pink), 'Golden Wedding' (yellow), 'Iceberg' (white), 'Intrigue' (dark red), 'Korresia' (bright yellow), 'Margaret Merril' (blush white), 'The Times Rose' (dark crimson) and 'Trumpeter' (orange-red).

• Half-standard roses are budded on to stocks 75cm (2½ft) above the ground and when mature are 1.3–1.6m (4½–5½ft) high. Varieties to choose from include: 'Amber Queen' (amber-yellow), 'Fellowship' (orange-embers), 'Golden Years' (golden), 'Korresia' (bright yellow), 'Margaret Merril' (blush white), 'Paul Shirville' (soft salmon-pink), 'Remembrance' (scarlet), 'Royal William' (deep red), 'Savoy Hotel' (light pink) and 'Silver Jubilee' (pink).

• Patio standards are budded on to stocks 75cm (2½ft) high and form dense, rounded heads packed with flowers over a long period of summer and into autumn. Varieties to choose from include: 'Cider Cup' (peach), 'Honeybunch' (bi-colour), 'Muriel' (pink), 'Red Rascal' (red), 'Sweet Dream' (peach) and 'Sweet Magic' (orange).

LEFT 'Intrigue' is a Floribunda with small to medium size, dark-red flowers borne in very showy clusters amid bushy growth. It was introduced in 1980. Do not confuse this red-flowered rose with a reddish-purple variety raised in North America and introduced in 1984.

LEFT 'Ballerina', a Hybrid Musk rose, is normally grown as a shrub, about 1.2m (4ft) high and wide. It can also be trained to form a standard rose; the light-pink, white-centred flowers are long-lasting.

ABOVE 'Centenaire de Lourdes' is a light soft-pink Floribunda with medium green leaves. It can be trained to grow as a standard.

RIGHT 'Troika', also known as 'Royal Dane', was introduced in 1972. It has large, fragrant flowers packed with orange-bronze shaded red petals. It grows vigorously to a height of 90cm (3ft), 75cm (2½ft) wide. This rose is resistant to diseases and the flowers do not fade.

ABOVE 'Rose Excelsa', also known as 'Red Dorothy Perkins', is usually grown as a Rambler but it also makes an excellent weeping standard. It has small double crimson flowers with white centres.

ABOVE Introduced in 1978, 'Silver Jubilee' is a universally acclaimed rose that has received many awards. It has scented, salmon-pink petals and grows to 75cm (2½ft). It has disease-resistant leaves.

- Miniature standards are grown on stems only 50cm (20in) high and when mature the head is about 90cm (3ft) tall. Varieties to choose from include: 'Baby Masquerade' (bi-colour), 'Colibri '79' (orange and apricot), 'Orange Sunblaze' (scarlet) and 'Pink Sunblaze' (pink).

- Weeping standards are grown on stems 1.3m (51in) high and when mature the heads are 1.5–1.8m (5–6ft) high. They have stems which cascade and create a magnificent display. Varieties to choose include: 'Albéric Barbier' (cream), 'Crimson Showers' (red), 'Dorothy Perkins' (rose-pink) and 'François Juranville' (salmon-pink), 'New Dawn' (blush) and 'Sanders' White' (white).

- Small trailing standards are increasingly popular, on 1m (39in) high and maturing to about 1.3m (4½ft) high. Varieties include 'Nozomi' (blush) and 'Suma' (red).

- Shrubby standards are grown on 1m (39in) high stems and provide plenty of colour. Varieties to choose from include 'Ballerina' (light pink), 'Canary Bird' (golden-yellow) and 'Bonica' (pink).

- Ground-cover roses are sometimes grown on stems 1m (39in) high and come in a range of colours. Varieties include: 'Gwent' (yellow), 'Hertfordshire' (carmine), 'Kent' (white), 'Suffolk' (crimson), 'Surrey' (clear pink) and 'Wiltshire' (rose-pink).

LEFT Planting Miniature roses in a container is an ideal way to display them as a group.

ABOVE 'Iceberg' is a fragrant, white Floribunda rose that has large blooms borne in trusses. It flowers throughout summer, often until the onset of winter.

MINIATURE ROSES

These fascinating roses, with small flowers and a miniature stature can be used in many ways, from edging borders to being planted in window boxes. Sometimes they are grown in pots and taken indoors while in bloom. But they are not houseplants and must be soon returned outdoors so that their stay in a warm, dry environment is limited to a few days at any one time.

Miniature roses have always been more popular in North America than in Britain, although they were developed in Europe, in particular Switzerland. It is said that in 1918, Dr Roulet, a surgeon in the Swiss Army, was so impressed by a rose growing in a pot near a cottage in Mauborget, Switzerland, that he enquired about its history. Local people told him that it bloomed throughout the year and had come from France about a century earlier. Henri Correvon, a Swiss alpine plant authority, was told and went in search of the rose. He discovered the village had burned down but cuttings were obtained from a neighbouring village. In 1922 it was introduced as *Rosa rouletii*; botanically it is similar to *R. chinensis* and is now known as *R. c.* 'Rouletii'. Much of the early work in developing Miniature roses was undertaken in Holland and Spain, where the colour range

MINIATURE ROSES FOR WINDOW BOXES

Miniature roses are excellent for planting in window boxes, where they create a display throughout much of the summer. Ensure that the compost in the box does not become dry through neglect, nor waterlogged because rain drips on it from gutters. Regularly remove dead flowers to encourage the development of further blooms. In winter, move the box to a sheltered position to prevent damage from strong winds.

BELOW 'Stars 'n' Stripes' has distinctive flowers, striped white and strawberry red, with prominent gold stamens. The bushes are about 30cm (12in) high and 38cm (15in) wide.

'Blue Peter' creates distinctive, small, lavender-purple flowers (right) which are borne on upright bushes about 35cm (14in) high and 30cm (12in) wide. It forms a superb Miniature rose and creates a spectacular display in gardens left. Unfortunately, the flowers have little scent.

was greatly extended while still keeping the miniature style of scaled-down buds, flowers, petals, stems and leaves. Few Miniature roses grow above 38cm (15in) high and it is the miniature appearance of the flowers and plants that separates them from Patio roses, which are low-growing forms of Floribunda roses. Miniature roses grow well in the same type of soil as other types, but take care when planting them in borders – perhaps as edgings – not to space them too far apart so that a great amount of soil is visible. Position them about 30cm (12in) apart; for small ones 20cm (8in) is better.

CLIMBING MINIATURE ROSES

There are few climbing Miniature roses, the best known one being 'Pompon de Paris, Climbing'. Its origin is uncertain, but it is thought to be a climbing form of the Miniature rose 'Pompon de Paris', well known in Victorian times and thought by some rose authorities to be *Rosa roulettii*. The climbing form which is grown today reaches about 2.1m (7ft) high and up to 2.7m (9ft) wide. It has masses of small, rose-pink, pompon-like flowers during the early part of mid-summer. These appear amid attractive, greyish-green leaves.

ABOVE 'Bush Baby' forms a small bush only 25cm (10in) high and wide. During summer it becomes packed with small, light salmon-pink blooms amid bushy growth. It was introduced in 1986 and the flowers are only slightly scented.

'Cinderella' develops small, slightly scented, white flowers tinged a delicate pink. They are borne in clusters on bushes only 30cm (12in) high and wide and amid shiny-green leaves. The stems are thornless and upright, making it ideal for planting in window boxes. The flowers have the bonus of lasting a long time when cut for use in flower arrangements indoors. It is the progeny of the China Rose 'Cécile Brünner' (also known as the 'Sweetheart Rose') and 'Peon'.

MINIATURE ROSE VARIETIES

Several Miniature roses are featured on pages 68 and 69. In addition to the ones illustrated, others to consider include:

* 'Baby Darling': Orange to pink flowers; 30cm (12in) high and 25cm (10in) wide.
* 'Baby Gold Star': Bright-yellow flowers; 30cm (12in) high and wide.
* 'Baby Sunrise': Glowing shades of orange and yellow flowers; 30cm (12in) high and wide.
* 'Cinderella': White flowers tinged delicate pink; 30cm (12in) high and wide.
* 'Dresden Doll': A superb miniature Moss rose with pink flowers; 30cm (12in) high and 23cm (9in) wide.
* 'Easter Morning': Large and ivory-white flowers; 38cm (15in) high and 25cm (10in) wide.
* 'Fire Princess': Orange-scarlet flowers with a touch of gold; 38cm (15in) high and 30cm (12in) wide.
* 'Lavender Jewel': Pink flowers flushed with lavender; 30cm (12in) high and wide.
* 'Mr Bluebird': lavender-blue flowers; 30cm (12in) high and 23cm (9in) wide.
* 'New Penny': Orange-red to copper-pink flowers; 25cm (10in) high and wide.
* 'Peachy White' Flowers: Initially almost white, becoming peachy-pink as they develop; 30cm (12in) high and wide.
* 'Red Ace': Dark-crimson flowers; 30cm (12in) high and wide.
* 'Rise 'n' Shine': Also known as 'Golden Sunblaze'. Unfading yellow flowers; 45cm (18in) high and 38cm (15in) wide.
* 'Scarlet Gem': Variable scarlet and very bright flowers; 25cm (10in) high and wide.
* 'Silver Tips': Pink flowers with a silver reverse, becoming soft lavender; 30cm (12in) high and wide.
* 'Stars 'n' Stripes': Flowers striped white and strawberry-red; 30cm (12in) high and wide.
* 'Sweet Fairy': Light-pink flowers; 30cm (12in) high and 25cm (10in) wide.
* 'Toy Clown': White flowers, shaded red at the edges; 30cm (12in) high and wide.
* 'Yellow Doll': Light yellow flowers; 30cm (12in) high and 23cm (9in) wide.

ABOVE 'Baby Masquerade', introduced in 1956 and also known as 'Baby Carnival', grows about 45cm (1½ft) high and 38cm (15in) wide. The slightly fragrant, yellow to pink and red flowers are borne in clusters amid bushy, dense growth. To encourage the development of new flowers, regularly remove the dead ones.

'Angela Rippon' bears clusters of rosy salmon-pink flowers amid bushy growth on plants 45cm (1½ft) high and 30cm (12in) wide. The flowers are fragrant and it was introduced in 1978.

LOOKING AFTER MINIATURES

Miniature roses can fill gardens with colour throughout most of summer, well into autumn and occasionally early winter. They can be grown in pots, tubs and window boxes as well as in gardens. In containers, use good soil-based compost and choose pots at least 30cm (12in) deep. Put coarse drainage material in the base of the container.

The soil must never be allowed to become dry and the roses should be fed every five to six weeks with a weak liquid fertilizer during their growing period. Stop feeding in the early part of late summer. Miniature roses have small root systems which are soon damaged by the use of strong fertilizers and excessive or neglectful watering.

Pests and diseases are frequently a major problem and plants must be sprayed regularly to prevent a small, insignificant outbreak becoming a catastrophe.

Very little pruning is needed, other than cutting out dead, diseased and spindly shoots, then trimming to form an attractive shape. Burn all diseased shoots to reduce the risk of further infection. If a small pair of secateurs is not available, use strong scissors.

ABOVE 'Top Marks' is sometimes listed as a Miniature rose but really it is a Patio type, which means it is a small Floribunda. Nevertheless, it is very attractive and displays clusters of small, vivid orange-vermilion flowers on bushes about 15cm (38in) high and 45cm (18in) wide. The flowers, which have little scent, are borne amid masses of shiny-green leaves.

'Orange Sunblaze' creates a vivid display of small, orange-red blooms on leafy plants 30cm (12in) high and wide. This is a French Miniature rose and was introduced in the 1980s.

RIGHT 'Anna Ford', introduced in 1980 and still considered superb, bears vivid orange-red flowers with a yellow base. They are borne in clusters amid dark-green, semi-glossy leaves and on plants 45cm (18in) high and 38cm (15in) wide. The flowers have slight fragrance and the plant, in general, has good resistance to diseases.

RIGHT 'Robin Redbreast' has small, almost single, currant-red flowers with pale centres. Bushes are full of small, shiny leaves, with a spreading habit and 45cm (1½ft) high and up to 60cm (2ft) wide. It was introduced in 1984 and it brings a blaze of colour to the beds in which it is planted.

PATIO ROSES

This is a relatively new group of small roses. Correctly, they are low-growing Floribunda roses and are ideal for planting around the edges of patios and terraces, where some of the more vigorous varieties would be too dominant. They are suitable for planting in beds, as well as in tubs and planters.

Most of these Patio roses are between 45cm (1½ft) and 60cm (2ft) high, although a few are 38cm (15in). They are hardier and more robust than the true Miniature roses, have bushy growth and a repeat-flowering nature.

In some rose books and catalogues, Patio roses have become a separate section, while in others they are listed with Floribunda roses and their dwarf nature indicated. In a few catalogues they are merged with the true Miniatures, so you can become involved in unnecessary detective work to find the roses you want. Dwarf Polyanthas are also sometimes merged with them, but in this book they are featured separately, on pages 74 and 75. However Patio, Miniature and Dwarf Polyantha roses are classified, they are superb plants for small gardens.

'Yellow Parade' is a Miniature rose with medium-yellow flowers, growing to a maximum of 40cm (16in) high. It was raised by Poulsen in 1990 and is also known as 'Rainbow Yellow Parade'.

'Bright Smile', also known as 'Dicdance' and introduced in 1980, has medium-sized, slightly fragrant, bright-yellow flowers borne amid bushy growth on plants 45cm (18in) high and wide. Initially, its bright qualities were not admired, but increasingly it is becoming popular and widely recommended. The bushes are vigorous and show good resistance to the onset of diseases.

'Sweet Magic' is a dwarf, cluster-flowered Patio rose with orange flowers attractively tinted gold. As well as growing Patio standard roses in borders, they also look very attractive in large pots and can be positioned on balconies and terraces. Part of their charm is the rounded head densely covered with petals.

OTHER PATIO ROSES

In addition to the Patio roses illustrated here, there are many others, including:

• 'Audrey Gardner': Flowers continuously throughout summer, with masses of bright-pink flowers; 45cm (1½ft) high.

• 'Bianco': Pure white, pompon-like flowers borne on bushy plants; 38–45cm (15–18in) high.

• 'Caroline Davidson': Rose-pink flowers with pale centres; 38cm (15in) high.

• 'Cider Cup': Small, deep-apricot, Hybrid Tea-shaped flowers; 38–45cm (15–18in) high. Only slightly scented.

• 'Dainty Dinah': Coral-pink flowers; 45–60cm (1½–2ft) high. Lightly scented.

• 'Esther's Baby': Bright rosy-pink, rather star-like flowers; 38cm (15in) high.

• 'Fairy Changeling': Deep-pink, rosette-shaped flowers; 45cm (1½ft) high.

• 'International Herald Tribune': Semi-double, rich-violet flowers edged purple; 60cm (2ft) high.

• 'Peek-a-Boo': Small, apricot flowers in graceful sprays; 45cm (1½ft) high.

• 'Petit Four': Semi-double, clear-pink flowers borne in showy clusters amid bush growth; 38cm (15in) high. It is only lightly scented.

• 'Pink Posy': Rosy-pink flowers with a sweet fragrance; 60cm (2ft) high.

• 'Sweet Dream': Apricot-peach flowers; 45cm (1½ft) high. Lightly scented.

• 'Wee Jock': Scarlet-crimson flowers; 38cm (15in) high. It has a light scent and masses of small, very attractive, dark leaves.

ABOVE 'Cottage Garden' produces deep-apricot flowers amid dark foliage on upright bushes 60cm (2ft) high and 45cm (1½ft) wide. Unfortunately, it is only lightly scented.

'Ocaru' is a miniature, fragrant, salmon-pink Patio rose. It is a cross between 'Rosy Jewel' and 'Zorina'.

DWARF POLYANTHA ROSES

These contributed to the mixture of rose genes which created the Floribundas, although now having little resemblance to them. True Dwarf Polyanthas are characterized by their bushy and compact nature, seldom exceeding 45cm (1¹/₂ ft) high, although many modern Dwarf Polyanthas are 90cm (3ft) tall. They form tough bushes, ideal for planting in borders, rose beds or in tubs and pots.

The first Polyantha Pompon appeared in 1875, when *R. multiflora* was crossed with *R. chinensis*. The result was 'Pâcquerette', an almost pure white variety, its recurrent-flowering nature derived from its pollen parent *R. chinensis*.

Floribunda roses owe their development to the Danish rose-breeder Svend Poulsen who, in the early 1920s, created a sensation throughout the rose world, particularly in England and North America, with the introduction of 'Else Poulsen' and 'Kirsten Poulsen'. They were originally known as Hybrid Polyantha roses, but later, after repeatedly crossing them with Hybrid Tea roses they were called Floribundas. The first one to be given this name was 'Rochester', which was raised in 1934 from a cross between the Hybrid Tea 'Rev. F. Page-Roberts' and 'Echo', a dwarf sport of the Rambler 'Tausendschön'.

Polyantha roses have therefore played an important role in the development of garden roses, as well as being delightful garden plants in their own right, and they are superb in containers placed on a patio.

ABOVE 'Baby Faurax', introduced in 1924, is still widely grown and cherished for its small, deep blue-purple flowers – some experts claim they are lavender-violet or even just violet – with a lighter base. The flowers are borne in clusters on plants 30–38cm (12–15in) high and wide. The flowers have little scent.

'Margo Koster', introduced in 1931, has small, open, cup-shaped, salmon-pink flowers borne on plants 45cm (1¹/₂ ft) tall. Sometimes its colour is described as orange-red. Earlier it was known as 'Sunbeam' and is said to be a sport from 'Greta Kluis'.

LEFT 'Coral Cluster', which was introduced in 1920, has large clusters of small, bright coral-pink flowers with yellow at the base of the petals. It grows about 45cm (1½ft) high. Coral Cluster is thought to be a sport from the 'Orleans Rose' which was introduced in France in 1909 and provided many other varieties. In the 1950s, individual flowers and trusses were reported reverting to their parent's nature, but this seldom occurs now.

OTHER DWARF POLYANTHA ROSES

✽ 'Gloire du Midi': Small, slightly fragrant, vivid orange-scarlet, pompon-like flowers on bushes about 45cm (1½ ft) tall. Introduced in 1932.

✽ 'Katharina Zeimet': Fragrant, pure white flowers borne in large clusters on short stems. Bushes are about 60cm (2ft) high. Introduced in 1901.

✽ 'Marie-Jeanne': Small, blush-cream flowers borne in large clusters. It is larger than most Dwarf Polyanthas, about 75cm (2½ft) high. Introduced in 1913.

✽ 'Marie Pavié': Twiggy bushes bearing clusters of blush-white flowers. Bushes grow about 45cm (1½ ft) high. Introduced in 1888.

✽ 'Nypel's Perfection': Hydrangea-pink flowers borne on vigorous bushes about 60cm (2ft) high. Introduced in 1930.

'Yesterday' has small, Rambler-like flowers. They are sweetly scented, rose-pink to lilac-pink and borne in graceful sprays. It was introduced in 1974 and grows about 90cm (3ft) high.

GROUND-COVER ROSES

The County Series of ground-cover plants has introduced a new dimension to the rose world in recent years and they have been hailed as a major breakthrough. It is too much to expect them to inhibit the growth of all weeds, especially if the ground is plagued with perennial types. Rather, these roses create a magnificent blanket of colour from the latter part of early summer to the middle of autumn. In addition to the County Series varieties featured below, other varieties include:

- 'Essex': Rich reddish-pink flowers; 60cm (2ft) high and 1.2m (4ft) wide.
- 'Gwent': Bright lemon-yellow flowers; 45cm (1$^{1}/_{2}$ft) high and 90cm (3ft) wide.
- 'Hampshire': Glowing-scarlet flowers; 30cm (12in) high and 60cm (2ft) wide.
- 'Suffolk': Bright-scarlet flowers; 45cm (1$^{1}/_{2}$ft) high and 90cm (3ft) wide.
- 'Warwickshire': Deep rose-red flowers; 45cm (1$^{1}/_{2}$ft) high and about 1m (3$^{1}/_{2}$ft) wide.
- 'Wiltshire': Deep rosy-pink flowers; 45cm (1$^{1}/_{2}$ft) high and 90cm (3ft) wide.

ABOVE 'Bonica', a Modern Shrub rose, grows about 75cm (2$^{1}/_{2}$ft) high and spreads up to 1.2m (4ft). It develops dainty clusters of small, rose-pink flowers.

'Norfolk' has masses of very fragrant, small to medium-sized, bright-yellow flowers in clusters on neat, bushy plants about 75cm (2$^{1}/_{2}$ft) high spreading to 90cm (3ft). It was introduced in 1990 and was the first yellow ground-cover plant in the County Series. It is an ideal ground-cover rose, forming sizeable 'hillocks' of colour. It can be planted in flower and shrub borders, towards the back or in the middle.

'Wiltshire' produces a magnificent display of reddish-pink flowers amid spreading stems and glossy leaves. The flowers are profuse, borne in large clusters on bushes 45–60cm (2ft) high and 90cm–1.2m (3–4ft) wide. It is ideal where late summer and early autumn colour is desired. The flowers have only a light scent, but the beautifully coloured, well-shaped flowers more than compensate for this. It was introduced in 1993.

MODERN SHRUB ROSES

Many of these roses can be used to create attractive ground cover. They are a comparatively recent development and display a profusion of large trusses of small, Rambler-like flowers on Shrub-like bushes. They are easy to grow. Some have a repeat-flowering nature, others flower just once but over a long period. In addition to those featured here, there are many others to consider, including:

• 'Bonica': Sprays or rose-pink flowers borne in dainty clusters; 75–90cm (2¹/₂–3ft) high and 1.2m (4ft) wide.

• 'Dentelle de Malines': Graceful and arching, with soft-pink, cup-shaped flowers; 1.2m (4ft) high and 1.5m (5ft) wide.

• 'Nozomi': Highly acclaimed, with pearly-pink to white flowers; 30–45cm (1–1¹/₂ft) high and 1.2–1.5m (4–5ft) wide.

LEFT 'Red Max Graf' is a red-flowered form of the pink-flowered Modern Shrub rose 'Max Graf'. 'Red Max Graf' reveals deep-red flowers on spreading and arching shrubs about 90cm (3ft) high and 1.8m (6ft) wide.

• 'Partridge': Low and ideal where a spreading shrub is needed. Pure white, single flowers; 30–45cm (1–1¹/₂ft) high and 1.2–3m (4–10ft) wide.

• 'Pleine de Grace': Impressive shrub with arching stems and large sprays of white, rambler-like flowers; 2.1m (7ft) high and 4.5m (15ft) wide. It is best restricted to large gardens.

• 'Raubritter': Superb and unique, with cupped, pink flowers; 90cm (3ft) high and 1.5m (5ft) wide.

• 'Red Blanket': Sprawling, with masses of small, rosy-red flowers; 75cm (2¹/₂ft) high and 1.5m (5ft) wide.

• 'Running Maid': Cupped, deep-pink flowers; 75cm (2¹/₂ft) high and 1.5–1.6m (5–6ft) wide.

• 'Smarty': Arching, with soft-pink flowers and a repeat-flowering nature; 90cm (3ft) high and 75cm (2¹/₂ft) wide.

• 'Snow Carpet': Superb, mound-forming shrub with small, double, white flowers from early summer to autumn; 30cm (12in) high and 75cm (2¹/₂ft) wide. It is only slightly scented but has glossy leaves.

'Scintillation', introduced in 1968, forms a large, sprawling shrub, 1.2m (4ft) high and about 1.8m (6ft) wide. It is ideal for climbing banks and as a hedge. The very fragrant, semi-double, blush-pink flowers are borne in large clusters. The flowers appear only once, but over a long period. It is an excellent ground-cover shrub when a large and bold display is wanted to cover a large area.

HEDGES

Roses provide attractive alternatives to traditional privet and yew hedges, although they do not have an all-green appearance throughout the year. Rose hedges, like traditional hedges, can be used to mark boundaries and to create divisions within a garden to separate one part from another. Robust varieties, such as Rugosas and Hybrid Briars, which are armed with prickles, are best used along the edges of properties; smaller, less thorny ones planted inside a garden. Rose hedges do not grow to a uniform height and width; they have a natural cottage-garden informality.

Remember that the width of rose hedges cannot be dramatically reduced and needs to be kept in check without spoiling them. They need yearly pruning to encourage the development of flowers over all their surface.

ROSES FOR HEDGES

Roses which are used to form hedges can be put into three groups, according to the height they will reach. To be effective, each bush must lose its individuality and form a continuous hedge, without bare patches.

When selecting a rose variety for planting as a hedge, choose one to suit the desired height. A range is listed here. Varieties used for tall hedges cannot be severely pruned to keep them small, as it is not their true nature and such pruning will not encourage the development of flowers – only strong stems that probably will be bare of blooms.

TALL HEDGES

These grow 1.5m (5ft) to 2.1m (7ft) high. Most are best as boundaries, but in a large garden they can be used to separate one part from another. Plant them 90cm (3ft) apart. Roses to choose from include:
• 'Blanc Double de Coubert': Rugosa rose with large, pure white, semi-double flowers almost continuously throughout summer.

ABOVE This hedge is formed of 'Masquerade', a vigorous Floribunda, that reveals masses of yellow to pink and flowers borne in showy clusters amid bushy growth. It is an ideal rose for forming a hedge and often grows 90cm (3ft) or more high It was introduced in 1949 and has remained popular ever since. As well as forming a hedge, it is ideal for planting in a mixed border.

- 'Buff Beauty': Hybrid Musk, with sturdy growth and large trusses of warm apricot-yellow flowers. Tea Rose scent.
- 'Canary Bird': Hybrid Shrub rose, with yellow flowers and fern-like leaves.
- 'Felicia': Hybrid Musk with silvery-pink flowers and strong fragrance. Has a bushy nature.
- 'Golden Wings': Modern Shrub rose, with large, scented, yellow flowers with mahogany-coloured stamens.
- 'Nevada': (*see below*).
- 'Penelope': (*see right*).
- 'Queen Elizabeth': Floribunda rose, with cyclamen-pink flowers. Plant 60–75cm (2–2^1/$_2$ft) apart.
- 'Roseraie de l'Hay': Rugosa, with crimson-mauve flowers.

MEDIUM HEDGES

These grow 75–1.5m (2^1/$_2$– 5ft) tall and are planted 45cm (1^1/$_2$ft) apart. If a wide hedge is needed, plant them in two rows, staggered and about 45cm (1^1/$_2$ft) apart. Varieties to seek include:

- 'Ballerina': Hybrid Musk with blossom-pink flowers.
- 'Celestial': An Alba rose with shell-pink flowers and golden stamens.
- 'Iceberg': Floribunda, with white flowers.
- 'Masquerade': Floribunda, with masses of yellow to pink to red flowers.
- 'Mountbatten': Floribunda, with yellow flowers.

SMALL HEDGES

These are under 75cm (2^1/$_2$ft) and are formed of short Floribunda, Patio, Dwarf Polyantha and Miniature types of roses. The planting distances vary, but are usually 30–38cm (12–15in) apart, although it may be necessary to adjust the spacings so that the foliage overlaps.

- 'Marlena': Patio rose with small, scarlet-crimson flowers throughout summer.
- 'The Fairy': Polyantha with rose-pink flowers.
- 'Trumpeter': Short Floribunda; orange-red flowers.

ABOVE 'Penelope' is a Hybrid Musk with a strongly branching nature and large trusses of fragrant, semi-double, pink flowers, flushed apricot and fading to creamy-white or light yellow. It has a repeat-flowering nature. Later it develops small, coral-pink fruits. It is ideal for forming a distinctive and eye-catching hedge about 1.5m (5ft) high.

LEFT 'Nevada' is a superb Modern Shrub rose with semi-double ivory-white flowers that become flushed pink in hot weather. They are about 10cm (4in) wide, with yellow stamens that become prominent when the flowers are fully open. Flowers appear in early summer and continue intermittently. As a hedge it reaches about 1.8m (6ft) high. Ensure its base does not become full of old shoots.

CLIMBERS AND RAMBLERS

Climbers and Ramblers can transform a garden with graceful flourishes of colour. They are superb for covering house walls, framing windows and doors, climbing on pillars, arches and pergolas, as well as scrambling into trees. Most gardens can benefit from them, especially small ones where ground space is limited. Indeed there is even a miniature-flowered climbing rose which although growing some 2.1m (7ft) high occupies very little garden space as it remains so close to the wall. Unsightly sheds and garages and old untidy hedges can be brightened by growing roses over them. They are also able to climb 1.6–2.4m (6–8ft) high poles, smothering them with flowers. This can be used to create tall beacons of colour which bring variety to the flatness of some garden borders. Pillar roses can also be featured in lawns to provide splashes of colour.

TYPES OF CLIMBING ROSES

There are basically two main types of these roses – Ramblers and Climbers.

• Rambler roses are mainly hybrids of *Rosa wichuraiana*, a low-growing shrub mainly from Japan and Korea, with flexible shoots which grow 3–3.6m (10–12ft) in one season. They have rosette-shaped flowers, borne in large trusses, and include well-known varieties such as 'Albéric Barbier', 'Crimson Shower', 'Dorothy Perkins' and 'François Juranville'.

Some later Ramblers have larger and more shapely flowers, but on more rigid growth and they lack the grace of earlier Ramblers. Nevertheless, they are impressive and include widely grown varieties such as the well-known 'Albertine', 'Emily Gray' and 'Paul's Scarlet Climber'.

• Climbers have a more permanent framework than Ramblers and include climbing sports of Hybrid Tea and Floribunda roses. There are also other types with diverse origins which include Climbing Tea roses, Climbing Bourbons and Noisette Climbers. In general, they all have stiffer stems but larger flowers borne in smaller trusses. Their framework is more or less permanent. Climbing roses include varieties such as 'Danse du Feu', 'Dortmund', 'Maigold', 'Meg', 'Mermaid' and 'Zéphirine Drouhin'. The climbing forms of Hybrid Teas include 'Ena Harkness, Climbing', 'Etoile de Hollande, Climbing' and 'Mrs Sam McGredy, Climbing'.

• Pillar roses include recurrent flowering climbers which have a restrained nature and grow 2.4–3m (8–10ft) high. They include varieties such as 'Aloha', 'Casino', 'Golden Showers' and 'New Dawn' (*see page 91*).

ABOVE 'Danse du Feu', introduced in 1953 and regarded as a Modern Climber because of its relatively recent introduction, has a repeat-flowering nature, with somewhat globular, semi-double, brilliant orange-scarlet flowers. It continues flowering well into autumn. Unfortunately, it has little fragrance and, with age, the flowers turn purple. But it is well worth growing, especially as it flourishes when planted against a cold, north-facing wall.
OPPOSITE The Sempervirens Rambler 'Félicité Perpétue' forms large clusters of small, creamy white flowers with primrose fragrance.

PRUNING CLIMBERS, RAMBLERS AND PILLAR ROSES

Ramblers and Climbers include such a wide range of roses, there is often confusion about the way they should be pruned. Basically, Climbers form a permanent – or, at least, a semi-permanent – framework of shoots. From these, lateral shoots (sideshoots) develop which bear flowers. These flowering lateral shoots develop in spring and summer and bear flowers during the same year. They should be pruned when the display of flowers is over. Ramblers have longer and more flexible shoots and do not create a permanent framework. The flowers are mainly borne on sideshoots which develop on the long stems produced during the previous year. When flowering is over, these long shoots should be completely cut out at the Rambler's base. Occasionally, a few of these older shoots are retained if the development of young shoots has not been prolific. There are a few Ramblers, such as 'Albertine', which do not produce masses of shoots from ground level but from higher up on the plant. In this case, shoots should be pruned back to these. At the same time it is necessary to retain some of the old wood.

CLIMBERS AND RAMBLERS

With both Climbers and Ramblers – but especially for the latter with their long, pliable stems – it is best to prune in late autumn or early winter, before they can be blown about and damaged by winter gales. Ramblers are best pruned at this time, but some rose enthusiasts (and especially those in cold areas) like to leave the pruning of Climbers until late winter or early spring. If this happens, always ensure shoots are tied to a framework in autumn to prevent strong winds causing damage. At the same time, check that support-ing wires or trellis are firmly secured and not likely to be blown down. If necessary, re-drill holes and insert new wall fixings. Strong wall fixings are essential as the weight of the stems and buffeting of winds can soon loosen them.

Pruning Climbers

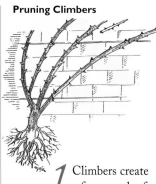

1 Climbers create a framework of shoots. Young, bare-rooted Climbers are delivered from nurseries between late autumn and late winter, when they are dormant. They will have three or four shoots up to 1.5m (5ft) long. Do not prune these back in the same way as when planting Ramblers (*see page 83*). Instead, just cut off weak sideshoots and tip back damaged tips. Trim back coarse and damaged roots. Plant the Climber firmly, in good soil, and spread out and train the shoots.

2 During the following spring and summer, shoots will develop from the framework. These must be tied to a trellis or wires. Ensure the stems are firmly secured but not strangled. It is essential to build up a strong framework. Some flowers will be borne at the tips of new shoots, as well as on lateral shoots which develop from the main framework. In late autumn, cut back laterals which have borne flowers to three or four eyes from their base. This radically reduces the amount of growth exposed to buffeting winds.

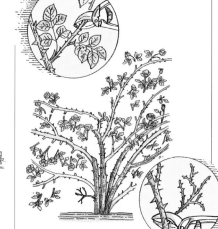

3 During the following year, the Climber will bear flowers on lateral shoots as well as the tips of young growths. During the following late autumn – and all subsequent years – cut back lateral shoots which have borne flowers to three or four eyes from their base. Also cut out weak and diseased shoots. Before the onset of windy winter weather, tie in shoots which have developed from the main stems. Occasionally, cut out old shoots at their base.

Pruning Ramblers

1 Plant young, bare-rooted Ramblers from late autumn to late winter, as soon as they arrive from a nursery. They will have three or four shoots, each perhaps as long as 1.2m (4ft). Use sharp secateurs to cut these back to 23–38cm (9–15in) long. Trim back coarse or damaged roots. Plant the Rambler firmly. During spring, young shoots will grow from the tops of shoots.

3 During the following summer, the Rambler will produce flowers. As soon as these have faded – usually during late summer and early autumn – use sharp secateurs to cut back to their bases all shoots that have borne flowers. At the same time, train in young shoots that developed earlier during the same season. These are the ones which will develop flowers on lateral shoots during the following season. Space out these shoots. Occasionally, insufficient new, young canes are produced; should this happen, only cut out the weakest and poorest and retain a few of the older and strong shoots which have just borne flowers. Cut their lateral shoots back to two or three eyes from the main shoot. Check that all shoots are firmly secured.

4 The Rambler will develop flowers during the following year. Always train and secure new shoots, training them horizontally if possible. Shoots at this angle develop flowers quicker than vertical ones. It also encourages the even development of lateral shoots along a stem's entire length. Do not allow shoots to remain loose to be blown about by the wind.

2 During summer, these young shoots will continue to grow, as well as others which develop from the Rambler's base. As they grow, train and loosely tie them into place. Ensure sufficient space is left for the stems to thicken. No flowers will be produced during the first year, as these are borne on lateral shoots which grow on the previous year's growths. Clearly, these do not exist during the first year after being planted.

PRUNING PILLAR ROSES

Roses grown against upright poles create attractive features. Plant suitable varieties (SEE PAGE 91) during their dormant period, from late autumn to late winter. Before planting pillar roses, always cut off weak and thin shoots.

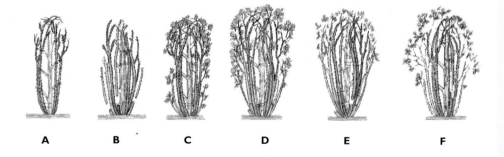

A   **B**   **C**   **D**   **E**   **F**

During the first year, young plants will develop long shoots. By autumn (sometimes earlier), they need to be loosely but firmly secured to the supporting pole (A). During the following summer, flowers develop. Cut these off when fading (B). Later, in early winter, cut back flowered laterals (C). At the same time, cut out dead, weak and old shoots (D). During the following summer, and all subsequent ones, cut out flowers when they fade (E). In early winter of the same year, and all further years, cut back flowered lateral shoots, as well as some of the new leading shoots (F).

CLIMBERS FOR ALL GARDENS

Climbing roses have larger flowers than the Ramblers and stiffer and more permanent growth. They also have the ability to repeat-flower after their first flowering period. There are several types of them: the Noisettes, Climbing Tea roses, Climbing Hybrid Tea and Climbing Bourbons are featured on pages 86 and 87. Here are the Modern Climbers, which have flowers with some resemblance to Hybrid Tea roses.

MODERN REPEAT–FLOWERING CLIMBERS

These are a relatively new group of Climbers; 'New Dawn' was introduced in 1930s, but most appeared during and since the 1960s. In addition to the superb varieties featured here, there are many others to consider, including:
• 'Breath of Life': Large, apricot to apricot-pink flowers on plants 2.7m (9ft) high and 2.1m (7ft) wide.
• 'Copenhagen': Large, deep-scarlet flowers borne on stiff, upright growth, 3m (10ft) high and 1.5m (5ft) wide.
• 'Coral Dawn': Large, double, deep coral-pink flowers on stiff, branching plants about 3.6m (12ft) high and 2.4m (8ft) wide.
• 'Handel': Small, semi-double, creamy-blush flowers rimmed rosy-red. Growth is upright and plants reach 3m (10ft) high and spread to 2.1m (7ft).
• 'Pink Perpétue': Large clusters of medium-sized, pink flowers with a carmine reverse. Plants are 2.7m (9ft) high and spreading to 2.4m (8ft).

LEFT 'Parade', a Modern Climber introduced in 1953, with an old-fashioned appearance. The petal-packed, strongly scented, dark-pink to carmine-red flowers are held in large clusters on stiff, branching stems. It is a tough and reliable climber, growing to about 3m (10ft) high and 2.4m (8ft) wide. It is ideal for growing as a pillar rose or against a wall or fence, but do not expect it to cover a high wall.

'Golden Showers' is one of the most freely flowering climbers, producing clusters of large, semi-double, scented, bright-yellow flowers on upright and branching growth. It is a Modern Climber, introduced in 1956 and a firm favourite of rose enthusiasts. It grows about 3m (10ft) high and 2.1m (7ft) wide and looks superb when planted at the side of a white-painted door. It can also be grown as a shrub in a border.

* 'Schoolgirl': Hybrid Tea-shaped, apricot-orange flowers on plants 3m (10ft) high and 1.8m (6ft) wide.

* 'Swan Lake': Fully-double, Hybrid Tea-like white flowers, tinged blush. Growth is stiff and branching, with deep-green leaves. About 3m (10ft) high and 1.8m (6ft) wide.

* 'Sympathie': Blood-red flowers borne in widely spaced clusters on stiff, branching growth. About 4.5m (15ft) high and 3m (10ft) wide.

* 'White Cockade': Large, double, milk-white flowers borne on stiff, branching plants about 2.1m (7ft) high and 1.5m (5ft) wide.

ROSES FOR COLD WALLS

Several climbers will survive when planted against walls that are shady and exposed to cold winds, including 'Gloire de Dijon' (buff-yellow/Noisette type), 'Mme Grégoire Staechelin' (glowing pink) and 'Mme Plantier' (white). There are also two Modern Climbers, 'Golden Showers' (golden-yellow and shown on the opposite page) and, especially, 'New Dawn' (silver blush-pink, and shown below).

Ramblers for cold walls include 'Albéric Barbier' (cream), 'Félicité et Perpétue' (creamy-white) and 'May Queen' (cupped and rose-pink).

SCENTED CLIMBERS

✳ 'Alchemist': Golden-yellow flushed orange.

✳ 'Compassion': Pink shaded apricot-orange.

✳ 'Crimson Glory, Climbing': Large and deep crimson.

✳ 'Ena Harkness, Climbing': Crimson-scarlet.

✳ 'Golden Showers': Bright yellow.

✳ 'Guinée': Richly dark-crimson.

✳ 'Kathleen Harrop': Soft pink.

✳ 'Lady Hillingdon, Climbing': Apricot-yellow.

✳ 'Lady Sylvia, Climbing': Blush-pink, suffused apricot.

✳ 'Mme Alfred Carrière': White, tinted pink.

✳ 'New Dawn': Silvery blush-pink.

✳ 'Sombreuil, Climbing': Creamy-white with pink centre.

✳ 'Sutter's Gold, Climbing': Gold flushed with pink.

ABOVE 'Compassion', a Modern Climber introduced in 1973, has well-shaped, Hybrid Tea-like pink flowers shaded apricot-orange. The stems are stiff and branching and clustered with masses of dark-green leaves. Its superb flowers are sweetly fragrant and borne on plants about 3m (10ft) high and 2.4m (8ft) wide. It is certainly one of the best of the Modern Climbers and one of the most popular.

'New Dawn' is one of the earliest Modern Climbers, introduced in 1930 and still a favourite. The medium-sized, silvery blush-pink flowers are fruitily fragrant and borne in large sprays on arching stems. It grows 3m (10ft) high and 2.4m (10ft) wide. It is the earliest to flower and most recurrent of all Modern Climbers. It is a sport from 'Dr W. Van Fleet' and is ideal as a pillar rose.

LEFT 'Zéphirine Drouhin', like
'Gloire de Dijon', is an Old rose and
recorded as being introduced in
1868. It is a Bourbon-type Climber,
with masses of fragrant, deep rose-
pink flowers throughout summer on
arching growth, 3–3.6m (10–12ft)
high and 1.8–2.4m (6–8ft) wide. It is
quite happy growing on a north-
facing wall and as well as being
planted as a Climber will grow in
a shrub border.

CLIMBING ROSES

In addition to the Modern
Climbers on pages 84 and 85,
there are others with older
parentage, some dating back to
the mid-1800s. They can be
put into four main groups,
though there are others.
The main ones are:
• Climbing Bourbons:
Although there are only a few
climbers in this group, they are
significant for their Old-rose
look and repeat-flowering
nature. They are hardy and

OTHER CLIMBERS TO CONSIDER

✳ 'Aimée Vibert': Pure white flowers with yellow stamens;
4.5m (15ft) high.

✳ 'Allen Chandler': Brilliant-crimson flowers with golden
stamens; 4.5m (15ft) high.

✳ 'Blairi No. 2': Deep-pink flowers, paling towards the edges;
4.5m (15ft) high.

✳ 'Blush Noisette': Semi-double, lilac-pink flowers, paling at
edges; 4.5m (15ft) high.

✳ 'Cécile Brünner, Climbing': Light-pink flowers; 3.6m
(12ft) high. Resistant to diseases.

✳ 'Céline Forestier': Silky, pale yellow and Tea Rose-scented
flowers; 2.4m (8ft) high.

✳ 'Etoile de Hollande, Climbing': Deep-crimson and highly
scented flowers; 5.4m (18ft) high.

✳ 'Guinée': Large, dark crimson with a strong fragrance;
4.5m (15ft) high.

✳ 'Mme Alfred Carrière': White, blush-tinted flowers; 5.4m
(18ft) high.

✳ 'Mme Grégoire Staechelin': Large, glowing-pink flowers;
6m (20ft) high.

✳ 'Maigold': Semi-double and bronze-yellow flowers amid
glossy leaves; 6m (20ft).

✳ 'Mermaid': Large, single, sulphur-yellow flowers with
amber stamens; 7.5–9m (25–30ft) high.

✳ 'Souvenir de Claudius Denoyel': Large and cupped, bright-
crimson flowers; 5.4m (18ft) high. It is widely acclaimed as
one of the best crimson-flowered climbers.

ABOVE A vigorous branching
grower, 'Maigold' is best grown up a
wall or fence. Reaching up to 3.7m
(12ft) it has large, bronze-yellow
flowers that appear in early
summer. It is powerfully fragrant.

include varieties such as the unusually named 'Blairii No. 2', introduced in 1845.

• Climbing Hybrid Teas: These are usually sports from bush varieties and reveal large, striking flowers. There are many fine examples of them, including 'Ena Harkness, Climbing', 'Etoile de Hollande, Climbing' and 'Lady Sylvia, Climbing'.

• Climbing Tea roses: These have a much older parentage than the Hybrid Tea-type Climbers, which they helped to create. They also have some similarity to the Noisettes. Climbing Tea roses include 'Lady Hillingdon, Climbing', 'Mrs Herbert Stevens, Climbing' and 'Paul Lédé'. Unfortunately, there are now few varieties to choose from.

• Noisette climbing roses: These, like the Bourbons, are Old roses, with subtle, delicate colouring. Their flowers are borne in rosettes on plants with long, slender shoots. Varieties within this group include the magnificent 'Alister Stella Gray', 'Aimée Vibert', 'Desprez à Fleur Jaune', 'Blush Noisette', 'Bouquet d'Or' and 'Céline Forestier'.

• Other climbers include 'Fellenberg' (a Climbing China type with clusters of small, deep-pink flowers), 'Iceberg, Climbing' (a form of the white-flowered Floribunda 'Iceberg'), and the Miniature rose 'Pompon de Paris, Climbing', which is discussed below, and is certainly the best known and widely grown of its type.

CLIMBING MINIATURE ROSE

'Pompon de Paris, Climbing' is a Miniature Climber, growing about 3m (10ft) high and 2.4m (8ft) wide and bearing clusters of small, dainty, pompon-like and double, red flowers on arching stems early during the rose season. These flowers are borne amid greyish green leaves. It is often a surprise that a rose classified as a Miniature can grow 3m (10ft) high, but it is the miniature nature of the flowers that gives its classification. It is thought to be a sport of 'Pompon de Paris', a Miniature Bush rose known in 1839 and earlier claimed to be a synonym of *Rosa roulettii*.

'Pompon du Paris, Climbing'

'Sympathie', a Modern repeat-flowering Climber, produces a mass of Hybrid Tea-like, velvety-crimson flowers on plants up to 3m (10ft) high. It was introduced in 1964.

RAMBLERS FOR ALL GARDENS

Rambling roses have a wide range of origins; most of them have quite clear parentage and are easily classified, others are less well known. Throughout the pages devoted to Ramblers (*pages 88 to 91*), their derivation is indicated when it is known. The main groups of Rambler roses are:

* Multiflora Hybrids: these Ramblers develop rather stiff growth and bear their flowers in large trusses. They can be described as typical Ramblers and many have a rich, musk-like fragrance. Ramblers of this type include 'Bobbie James' (*below right*), 'Goldfinch' (*far right*), 'Rambling Rector' and 'Rose-Marie Viaud'.

* Sempervirens Hybrids: these have a graceful nature, with sprays of small flowers borne on long, slender stems. They are hardy and once established create a mass of trailing stems and flowers. This type includes a wide range of Ramblers, such as 'Adélaide d'Orléans', 'Félicité et Perpétue' (*opposite page*) and 'Princesse Louise'.

ABOVE 'Goldfinch' has clusters of button-like, yellow flowers which with age become white. It is a Multiflora type and grows about 3m (10ft) high.

LEFT 'Albéric Barbier' is a Wichuraiana Rambler, well known for its yellow buds which open to reveal creamy-white flowers. These have the bonus of a fresh fruit fragrance.

'Bobbie James', introduced in 1961 is a splendid Multiflora Hybrid. It has large clusters of small, semi-double, very fragrant, glistening creamy-white flowers. It grows 9m (30ft) high and about 6m (20ft) wide and is ideal for covering pergolas, unsightly sheds and garages, and it is also very good for climbing into trees. As an added advantage, the leaves are a beautiful polished-copper shade.

ABOVE 'Félicité et Perpétue', a Sempervirens type, creates showy clusters of rosette-style, creamy-white flowers which reveals a delicate primrose fragrance. It grows 4.5–6m (15–20ft) high and 3.5–4.5m (12–15ft) wide. Few climbers are so reliable and free-flowering as this 1827 introduction, although it is not repeat-flowering and blooms only in mid-summer.

• Wichuraiana Hybrids: a major group of rambling roses, with sprays of large flowers borne in elegant sprays on graceful growths. Many varieties have a rich, apple-like fragrance and magnificent flowers. Examples of this group include: 'Albéric Barbier', 'Albertine' (*below*), 'American Pillar', 'Crimson Shower', 'François Juranville', 'Paul Transon' and 'Sanders' White'.

• There are a few other groups, that are not as well known as the previous three but they include some excellent Ramblers. An example of these is 'Mme de Sancy de Parabère', a Boursault type. 'Wedding Day' is a seedling variety of the species *Rosa sinowilsonii*, while the well-known 'Paul's Himalayan Musk' is thought to be a cross between *Rosa brunonii* and a Moschata Hybrid rose.

Other Ramblers to Consider

* 'Adélaïde d'Orléans': Sempervirens; small and semi-double, creamy-white flowers; 4.5m (15ft) high.
* 'Albéric Barbier': Wichuraiana; double and creamy-white flowers; 7.5m (25ft) high.
* 'Crimson Shower': Wichuraiana; bright-crimson flowers and dark foliage; 4.5m (15ft) high.
* 'Francis E. Lester': White flowers, petals tinted blush at their edges; 4.5m (15ft).
* 'François Juranville': Wichuraiana; rosy salmon-pink flowers; 4.5m (15ft).
* 'Gerbe Rose': Wichuraiana; peony-like fragrant, soft-pink flowers tinted cream; 3.6m (12ft) high.
* 'Paul Transon': Wichuraiana; coppery-orange flowers borne in small clusters; 4.5m (15ft) high.
* 'Paul's Himalayan Musk': spectacular sprays of blush-pink flowers; 9m (30ft) high.
* 'Princess Louise': Sempervirens; sprays of creamy-blush flowers; 3.6m (12ft).
* 'Sanders' White': Wichuraiana; small, semi-double, pure white flowers; 5.4m (18ft) high.
* 'The Garland': A cross between *R. moschata* and *R. multiflora*; creamy-salmon flowers; 4.5m (15ft) high.
* 'Veilchenblau': Multiflora; clusters of pale-lilac, white-centred flowers; 4.5m (15ft) high.
* 'Wedding Day': Large clusters of creamy-white to blush flowers; 7.5m (25ft) high.
* 'Weetwood': Vigorous, with pendulous sprays of pink flowers; 7.5m (25ft) high.

'Albertine', perhaps one of the best known Ramblers, was introduced in 1921. It is a Wichuraiana type and produces light salmon-pink flowers with a fruity fragrance in large clusters during the latter part of early summer, and often a later crop.

'Seagull', introduced in 1907 and a Multiflora Rambler, has a mass of highly scented, pure white, single flowers with golden stamens. It grows up to 6m (20ft) high and is ideal for introducing brightness into dull trees.

'Rambling Rector' is a Multiflora Rambler with vigorous, twiggy growth that becomes smothered with small, semi-double, creamy-white flowers. In autumn, these are followed by small hips (fruits).

ROSES TO GROW IN TREES

There are many Climbers and Ramblers, as well as Species types, which excel at climbing into trees and creating fine displays. Such roses do not have to be exceptionally vigorous. Indeed, some are only 3.6m (12ft) or so high. When planting them, prepare the site by replacing old soil. Water the plants regularly to ensure they become established quickly. This is because soil around the base of a tree is often impoverished and dry. Also feed them regularly.

No regular pruning is needed and once established there is nothing to do except to feed them a couple of times a year, during early and mid-summer. Varieties and species to consider include:

- 'Awakening': Blush; Climber; 3–3.6m (10–12ft).
- 'Bobbie James': Creamy-white; Rambler; 9m (30ft).
- 'Cécile Brünner, Climbing': light pink; Climber; 3.6–6m (12–20ft).
- 'Emily Gray': Butter-yellow; Rambler; 4.5m (15ft).
- 'Francis E. Lester': Blush to white; Rambler; 4.5m (15ft).
- 'Kiftsgate': Creamy-white; Climber; 9m (30ft).
- 'Leverkusen': Light yellow; Climber; 3–4.5m (10–12ft).
- 'Mme Grégoire Staechelin': Rosy carmine-pink; Climber; 6m (20ft).
- 'Paul's Himalayan Musk': Blush to lilac-pink; Rambler; 9m (30ft).
- *Rosa brunonii*: White; wild climbing species; 7.5m (25ft).
- *Rosa longicuspis*: Milky-white; wild climbing species; 7.5m (25ft).
- *Rosa soulieana*: Pale yellow, opening to white; wild climbing species; 3.6m (12ft).
- 'Seagull': White; Rambler; 6m (20ft).
- 'Sympathie': Blood-red; Climber; 4.5m (15ft).
- 'Veilchenblau': Opening dark magenta and fading to lilac; Rambler; 4.5m (15ft).
- 'Wedding Day': Creamy-white; Rambler; 7.5m (25ft).

'Kiftsgate', also known as *Rosa filipes* 'Kiftsgate', was introduced in 1954. It is very vigorous and soon reaches 9m (30ft) high and with a large spread. During the latter part of early summer and into mid-summer it produces scented, creamy-white flowers which are followed by small, oval fruits.

PILLAR ROSES

These are roses which have a restrained growth habit and grow 2.4–3m (8–10ft) high, some slightly higher. They are repeat-flowering and create colour over a long period. Some are Climbers, others Modern Climbers, Ramblers, Shrub roses or Modern Shrub roses. There are many varieties to choose from, including:

ABOVE 'Aloha', a Modern Shrub rose, is ideal as a low climber against a pillar. It was introduced in 1949, is robust and reveals very fragrant, clear-pink, cupped and old-fashioned flowers. It can also be grown in a shrub border but is more distinguished when grown as a pillar rose.

- 'Aloha': Modern Shrub rose; clear pink and repeat-flowering.
- 'Bantry Bay': Climber; deep pink; light scent.
- 'Compassion': Modern Climber; salmon-pink tinted apricot-orange.
- 'Copenhagen': Modern Climber; dark scarlet.
- 'Dreaming Spires': Climber; yellow, with good scent.
- 'Galway Bay': Modern Climber; salmon-pink.
- 'Golden Showers': Modern Climber; golden-yellow.
- 'Handel': Modern Climber; creamy-blush, edged pink.
- 'Highfield': Modern Climber; primrose-yellow.
- 'Kathleen Harrop': Climbing Bourbon; soft-pink.
- 'New Dawn': Modern Climber; silvery blush-pink.
- 'Phyllis Bide': Rambler; yellow, flushed salmon-pink.
- 'Pink Perpétue': Modern Climber; bright rose-pink.
- 'Reine Victoria': Bourbon Shrub; shell-pink.
- 'White Cockade': Modern Climber; pure white.
- 'William Allen Richardson': Noisette Climber; yellow with yolk-yellow centre.

'Bantry Bay', introduced in 1967 from a cross between the Modern Climber 'New Dawn' and 'Korona', has deep-pink flowers borne on upright plants, about 3.6m (12ft) high. It is ideal for growing as a pillar rose.

'Highfield', a Modern Climber introduced in 1980, has primrose-yellow flowers, borne freely and it is very fragrant. It grows about 3m (10ft) high and is ideal for growing as a pillar rose. If it is pruned severely, it can be grown as a shrub in a border when it is about 1.5m (5ft) high and wide. However, it is better when grown up a pillar. 'Highfield' is a sport of 'Compassion', another Modern Climber.

SUPPORTS FOR PILLAR ROSES

The simplest way to support a pillar rose is to dig a deep hole and to secure a long, thick pole in it. If several sideshoots of the pole have been left sticking out, these help to give rose stems something to nestle against. Alternatively, three planed pieces of wood about 2.4m (8ft) high can be erected like a wigwam, with a base about 1.2m (4ft) across. Whichever way the support is constructed, it must be strong enough to avoid toppling during strong winds.

SHRUB ROSES

Shrub roses is an all-embracing classification. It encompasses Species roses, which are native to many countries in the northern hemisphere and have been grown for several thousand years and it also includes some of their progeny. Species roses usually have single flowers, formed of five petals, although there are some double and semi-double forms. Some of this group, together with the new types of roses they formed, have become known as Old roses, but the demarcation between Species roses and Old roses is somewhat blurred. Old roses were specially cherished during the eighteenth and nineteenth centuries for their large, petal-packed flowers which were often beautifully scented. Old roses flower in profusion during the latter part of early summer and into mid-summer, but rarely again, although the autumn Damask and Portland types do bloom later. When the Modern Shrub roses were introduced, with their ability to flower over a longer period, many Old roses fell out of fashion.

Species roses include well-known types such as the Damask rose (*Rosa damascena*), Dog rose (*R. canina*) and sweetbriar or Eglantine (*R. rubiginosa*). Some of the natural and man-created crosses between Species roses are included in this grouping. Examples of these include forms of the Ramanas rose (*R. rugosa*) such *R. r.* 'Roseraie de l'Hay'. There are other examples of varieties being classified in the Species types, as well as the hybrid *R. × alba*. This is the 'white rose of York' and a natural cross between *R. gallica* (known as either the 'Provins rose' or 'French rose') and *R. canina*.

Old roses include the Albas, Bourbons, Centifolias, Chinas, Damasks, Gallicas, Hybrid Musks, Hybrid Perpetuals, Hybrid Sweetbriars, Moss, Portland, Scotch and Tea roses. All those Old roses – other than Species type – were present before the introduction of Hybrid Tea roses.

ABOVE The Centifolia rose 'Tour de Malakoff' creates a magnificent display, with large magenta-purple flowers that turn to a rich parma-violet before becoming lavender and grey. It forms a spectacular shrub about 1.8m (6ft) high and 1.5m (5ft) wide. OPPOSITE *Rosa × cantabrigiensis* also creates a feast of colour, with 6cm (2½in) wide pale-yellow flowers that nestle among fern-like foliage. It grows about 3m (10ft) high and wide.

The so-called Modern Shrub roses have a diversity of origins, but are mainly crosses between Modern Bush roses and stronger growing types such as Species and Climbers. They have an informal nature and most flower intermittently throughout summer. They include varieties such as 'Aloha', 'Frühlingsmorgen' and 'White Pet', a perpetual flowering sport of 'Félicité Perpétue', a Rambler rose. In addition to these, there are the Modern Shrub roses which are used as ground cover, and are featured on pages 104 and 105.

These new roses, with their ability to flower almost continuously throughout the rose year, have their value, but for many rose-growers they do not have the individuality and fragrance of the Old roses. A walk through any established garden planted with Old roses will convince you of their beauty and distinctive qualities which, for many rosarians, remain incomparable.

PRUNING SHRUB ROSES

Shrub roses need regular pruning to encourage the development of flowers each year and this also prevents congestion and ensures longevity. These shrubs are becoming increasingly popular and their natural appearance is a great part of their appeal.

Because many of them have been growing for thousands of years without the hand of man restraining them, it is often suggested that they should be left alone to grow naturally. This may suit some of them, but certainly not all. It may also be thought that all Shrub roses have the same habit and therefore need similar pruning, but this again is incorrect. As a way of simplifying pruning it is possible to put them into three main groups. In fact there are many roses that test these classifications and do not fit neatly into them. The three main ways to prune them are explained here, as well as indications of the types of roses that need particular treatment.

ABOVE 'Charmian', a new English rose, develops full-petalled, rich-pink flowers on bushes about 1m (3½ ft) high and wide.

GROUP ONE INCLUDES:
* Species roses (but not Climbers) and their close hybrids.
* Ramanas rose (*R. rugosa*) and its hybrids.
* Burnet rose (*R. pimpinellifolia/R. spinosissima*) and its hybrids.
* The French rose (*R. gallica*).
* Hybrid Musks, which bear flowers in large trusses.

INITIAL PRUNING
When roses are being planted during their dormant period, cut off coarse and weak roots. If any have been damaged, prune them back to where the root is sound. Also, shorten damaged and unripe shoots. During the first and second years cut out a few old shoots as well as diseased and thin ones, in winter.

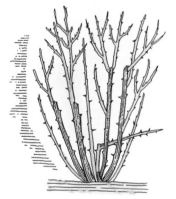

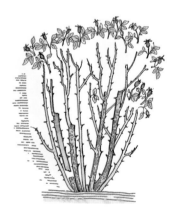

1 During late winter or early spring of the second year, completely cut off shoots that have developed from the plant's base and are badly positioned (*above*). Also, tip back vigorous shoots. During the subsequent summer, the plant will produce flowers on shoots borne on old wood.

2 During the same season, strong shoots will develop directly from the shrub's base. In early autumn, after the flowers have faded, cut out thin and weak growths, as well as those that have become damaged or diseased. Additionally, cut off the tip of each shoot.

3 During the third and subsequent years, regular winter pruning is essential. In late winter or early spring, cut back lateral shoots. Also, cut out at their base one or two shoots that are passed their best (*inset*). In mid- and late summer, the shrub will bear flowers on lateral shoots.

4 During early autumn, cut back the tips of shoots to encourage the development of laterals that will bear flowers during the following year. Also, cut out thin and weak shoots, and totally remove old ones at the shrub's base. It is essential that light and air enters the shrub.

GROUP TWO INCLUDES:
* *R. × alba* types.
* Provence rose (*R. centifolia*) and its types.
* Most Damasks (roses with *R. damascena*) in their make up.

* Moss roses.
* Also includes Modern Shrub roses which do not repeat-flower and have one main flush of bloom in mid-summer.

This group is formed of roses which flower mainly on short lateral shoots as well as sub-laterals originating from two-year-old wood – or older.

INITIAL PRUNING
When being planted, cut off coarse, damaged and weak roots and cut back diseased and thin shoots.

1 In late winter or early spring of the second year, cut back by about a third those shoots that developed earlier from the shrub's base. Additionally, cut back to two or three eyes all laterals that developed on flowered shoots.

2 During early and late autumn of the second year, tip back shoots that are extra long. By doing this, the risk of the shrub being damaged or its roots loosened by strong wind (usually known as wind-rock) is dramatically reduced.

3 In late winter and early spring of the third and subsequent years, cut back by a third new shoots that develop from ground level. Prune back laterals on flowered shoots to two or three eyes from their base and cut out a few old shoots.

4 Later in the same season – and all subsequent ones – use sharp secateurs to cut off the ends of shoots that are extra long. This reduces the area exposed to the buffeting of winds during winter. Also, the stems, if long, will whip against each other.

GROUP THREE INCLUDES:
* Most China roses.
* Most Bourbon roses.
* Modern Shrub roses, other than those detailed in Group Two and mainly with only one

flowering period during each year.
* Extremely vigorous and robust Hybrid Teas and Hybrid Perpetuals can also be included here.

INITIAL PRUNING
This is the same as in Group One. When planting, cut off coarse and weak roots, as well as those that may have been damaged during the shrub's

transit from a nursery. Also, prune back damaged and unripe shoots. During the first and second years, cut out a few old shoots as well as diseased or thin ones in winter.

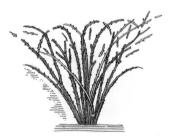

1 In late winter or early spring, cut back excessively long shoots that have developed from the shrub's base by about a third. Also, cut back laterals on shoots which flowered during the previous season to within two or three eyes of their base. Additionally, cut out weak shoots.

2 During the latter part of early summer and into mid-summer, shrubs in this section bear flowers on lateral shoots borne on the previous season's shoots. Summer-prune these by cutting off dead flower clusters. In late autumn, tip back long shoots to reduce the area exposed to wind.

3 In late winter or early spring of the third and subsequent years, cut back very long shoots that arise from the shrub's base by about a third. Also, cut back lateral shoots that flowered during the previous season to two or three eyes. Cut out weak and spindly shoots to their base.

4 In mid-summer of the third and subsequent years, the shrub will flower on lateral shoots developed during the previous year. When their display is over, summer-prune them by cutting off faded and dead flower clusters. When pruning shrubs in the group, encourage an arching habit.

SPECIES ROSES

Botanists have suggested that there are more than 3,000 species of roses. This may be an exaggeration as some botanists detect differences imperceptible to gardeners. As far as gardeners are concerned there are probably only 150 that are garden-worthy and have contributed to the wealth of roses grown today. The initial and continued success of Species roses lies in their hardiness, promiscuity and willingness to be domesticated. Many of them originated in harsh winter conditions, where a deciduous nature is essential for the survival of flowering plants. In addition, the ability of some roses to accept the natural transference of pollen between two different species and to produce hybrids has helped in concentrating into a potential parent the characteristics of several of them. Other Species roses developed sports, natural mutations in colour or growth, and these can be detached and used to create similar plants.

Until the marriage, during the end of the 1700s and early 1800s, between roses from China and those from western Asia (by that time often called European roses because of their long association with that area), the Species roses and their natural offspring were the only roses grown in Europe. Many of these 'European' roses were initially brought to Europe as spoils of war and particularly collected for their fragrance or medicinal value.

ABOVE *Rosa × headleyensis*, raised in about 1920 from parents and thought to be *R. hugonis* and *R. sericea*, develops strongly fragrant, creamy-yellow flowers among fern-like foliage and on plants 2.7m (9ft) high and 3.6m (12ft) wide. It forms a superb feature in a large garden and is a fine example of a man-made cross between two species.

GALAXY OF SPECIES

To describe all the Species roses in this limited space is impossible. The following species are chosen to indicate their variety and to create interest in them.

- The Damask rose (*Rosa damascena*) belongs to a group introduced from the Middle East by returning Crusaders in the holy wars undertaken between 1096 and 1291. It has 7.5cm (3in) wide, fragrant, white flowers during early and mid-summer.
- The cabbage rose or rose of Provence (*R. centifolia*) is an ancient and sterile form of *Rosa gallica*. It has, however, produced many exciting sports, including 'Muscosa', the Moss rose which has resinous glands on its sepals and, sometimes, on its leaf-stalks.
- The French rose or Provins rose (*R. gallica*) should not confused with the Rose of Provence (*R. centifolia*). The French rose is native to southern Europe and western Asia and bears showy, purple-pink flowers up to 7.5cm (3in) wide during early summer. It has borne many sports, including 'Officinalis' (also known as the 'red rose of Lancaster' and 'Apothecary's rose'). The famous 'Versicolor', perhaps better known as 'Rosa Mundi', is a sport of 'Officinalis'.
- The Austrian Briar (*R. foetida*) is a suckering shrub from western Asia with strongly scented, buttercup-yellow flowers. It has played an important role in introducing yellow into later roses.
- The Ramanas rose (*R. rugosa* and often also known as the Japanese rose), from eastern Asia, reveals heavily scented, deep-pink flowers up to 7.5cm (3in) across. It has also produced many superb hybrids.

UNUSUALLY SCENTED SPECIES ROSES

✶ *R. canina* 'Andersonii': Deep-pink flowers; raspberry-drop fragrance.

✶ *R. davidii*: Mallow-pink flowers; peony-scented.

✶ *R. paulii*: Pure white flowers; rich clove fragrance.

✶ *R. pimpinellifolia* 'Double White': Small, globular, white flowers; lily-of-the-valley fragrance.

✶ *R. soulieana*: White flowers; sweet banana fragrance.

✶ *R. longicuspis*: Climber with single, white flowers; banana-like smell.

✶ *R. wichuraiana*: Rambler with clusters of white flowers; scent of green apples.

Rosa canina 'Andersonii' develops arching stems which have a raspberry-drop fragrance and intensely deep-pink flowers followed in autumn by bright orange-red, oval hips. It is thought to be a Gallica hybrid and forms a shrub about 1.8m (6ft) high and 2.4m (8ft) wide. *Rosa canina*, the well-known Dog rose, is native to Europe and the British Isles.

Rosa rubiginosa, the sweet-brier or eglantine and also early known as *R. eglanteria*, has been acclaimed in literature. The single, pink flowers are numerous and borne amid strongly aromatic foliage; the fragrance is most noticeable during damp evenings. It forms a thicket-like shrub, 2.4m (8ft) high and wide. The flowers are followed by red, oval hips.

ABOVE 'Celestial', also known as 'Céleste', is an Alba rose with semi-double, soft shell-pink flowers that are especially attractive when beginning to open. The flowers are shown to perfection by the grey leaves. It forms a shrub about 1.8m (6ft) high and 1.2m (4ft) wide.

OLD ROSES

It is easy to be enchanted by Old roses which, although at their most popular in the eighteenth and nineteenth centuries, have continued to be treasured by modern rose enthusiasts. They form hardy bushes, full of vigour and with richly coloured, petal-packed flowers. Some of the flowers are 'quartered', which means they have a flat centre and petals densely arranged in four groups. Most of these roses are superbly scented, which is a compensation for their relatively short flowering season. The Modern Shrub roses have a longer flowering season and are featured on pages 104 and 105. Old roses are ideal for planting in shrubberies and mixed borders, where they merge well with a variety of other plants.

The Old roses can be arranged into thirteen types, according to their derivation, although because some roses have a mixture of genes in them they can lay claim to two groupings. To make these groups easy to find, they are arranged in alphabetical order between here and page 103.

ALBA ROSES
These derive from *Rosa alba* and form vigorous, upright, hardy shrubs with pink, blush and white flowers, mainly during mid-summer. Varieties to consider include:
• 'Alba Maxima': Also known as the Jacobite rose and great double white, it has very fragrant, creamy-white, slightly untidy flowers; 1.8m (6ft) high and 1.5m (5ft) wide.
• 'Celestial': (*see page 97*).
• 'Félicité Parmentier': Densely packed buds opening to clear, fresh-pink flowers about 6cm (2^1/$_2$in) across; 1.2m (4ft) high and wide.
• 'Queen of Denmark': Soft glowing-pink and quartered; 1.5m (5ft) high and 1.2m (4ft) wide.

BOURBON ROSES
These have mainly China and Portland roses in their blood, as well as a medley of other Old roses. The flowers have an old-fashioned character, with excellent fragrance. Many varieties have a repeat-flowering habit and include:
• 'Boule de Neige': Silky textured, globular, double, ivory-white flowers; 1.8m (6ft) high and 1.2m (4ft) wide.
• 'Louise Odier': (*see below*).
• 'Mme Isaac Pereire': Large, richly fragrant, madder-crimson, cup-shaped flowers, reflexed at edges; 1.5m (5ft) high and 1.2m (4ft) wide.
• 'Souvenir de la Malmaison': Strongly fragrant, large, soft-pink flowers paling at their edges with age; 90cm (3ft) high and wide.

'Louise Odier', a Bourbon rose, forms a shrub 1.5–1.8m (5–6ft) high and 1.2–1.5m (4–5ft) wide. It has deliciously fragrant, perfectly formed, cup-like flowers of rich pink softly shaded with lilac and blooms almost continuously throughout the rose year. It was introduced in 1851 and has been popular ever since.

CENTIFOLIA ROSES

These are derived from *Rosa centifolia*, the rose of Provence and also known as the cabbage rose. They have fragrant flowers in clusters during mid-summer. Varieties include:
• 'Centifolia': Richly fragrant, deeply globular, clear pink flowers; 1.5m (5ft) high and 1.2m (4ft) wide.
• 'Chapeau de Napoleon': (*see below*).
• 'Fantin-Latour': Blush-pink, deepening to shell-pink at the centre; 1.8m (6ft) high and 1.5m (5ft) wide.
• 'Robert le Diable': Slate-grey splashed scarlet and cerise; 1.2m (4ft) high and 90cm (3ft) wide. Superb shrub.
• 'Tour de Malakoff': Magenta-purple, later parma-violet, grey and lavender; 1.8m (6ft) high and 1.5m (5ft) wide.

CHINA ROSES

These flower repeatedly throughout the rose season. Ensure they are given a sunny position and shelter from cold winds. Varieties include:
• 'Hermosa': Fragrant, globular, pretty little pink flowers; 90cm (3ft) high and 60cm (2ft) wide. Ideal for a small garden.
• 'Mutabilis': Well known for its continuous flowering nature, with flame-coloured buds which open to coppery-yellow and later coppery-crimson; 2.4m (8ft) high and 1.8m (6ft) wide.
• 'Old Blush China': (*see below*).
• 'Sophie's Perpetual': Small, deep-pink flowers borne in small sprays; 1.8m (6ft) high and 1.2m (4ft) wide. It is a variety with very few thorns.

MIXING AND MATCHING OLD ROSES

✻ 'Fantin-Latour', a Centifolia rose, has blush-pink flowers, deepening at their centre, which associate well with large, dull-yellow and light-green leaves of hostas. Ensure that the colours are subdued and do not dominate the rose.

✻ 'Queen of Denmark', an Alba type and also known as 'Königin von Dänemark', has quartered, glowing-pink flowers with a button-like eye. It associates well with the ornamental and flowering pear tree *Pyrus salicifolia* 'Pendula'. A few irregularly positioned lavenders could further enhance the front of the border, but take care they do not spread and eventually dominate the rose.

✻ 'Mme Isaac Pereire', a Bourbon rose, has large, madder-crimson flowers which harmonize with white lilies and soft-pink paeonies. It is essential to create a quiet informal setting. Strong dramatic colours and formal regular planting patterns are wrong for Old roses; relaxed, informal situations are best.

'Chapeau de Napoleon', a Centifolia rose introduced in 1826 and also known as *R. centifolia* 'Cristata' and 'Crested Moss', is easily mistaken for a Moss rose. The richly fragrant, pure-pink flowers are borne on plants 1.5m (5ft) high and 1.2m (4ft) wide.

'Old Blush China', introduced in 1789 and also known as 'Common Blush' and 'Blush China', as well as the 'Monthly Rose' because of the way it continues flowering to Christmas, has graceful clusters of pale-pink flowers. When planted against a warm wall it grows about 2.4m (8ft) high, but otherwise perhaps only 1.2m (4ft).

BELOW 'Ispahan', a Damask rose also known as 'Rose d'Isfahan' and 'Pompon des Princes', is one of the first of the Old roses to flower and one of the last to remain in bloom. Its neat buds open to reveal clear pink, very fragrant flowers. It forms a shrub about 1.5m (5ft) high and 1.2m (4ft) wide.

DAMASK ROSES

A group derived from *R. damascena* and revealing elegant foliage and, usually, scented flowers. The bushes have bristly and thorny stems, with grey-green leaves and flowers during mid-summer. Varieties include:
• 'Celsiana': Clusters of soft-pink flowers with golden stamens; 1.5m (5ft) high and 1.2m (4ft) wide.

• 'La Ville de Bruxelles': Very fragrant, fully-double, rich-pink flowers; 1.5m (5ft) high and 1.2m (4ft) wide.
• 'Marie Louise': Large, intensely pink flowers that begin by opening wide and flat, then arching; 1.2m (4ft) high and wide.
• 'Petite Lisette': Miniature, clear blush-pink, flat and circular flowers in open sprays; 1.2m (4ft) high and 90cm (3ft) wide.

GALLICA ROSES

These are derived from *R. gallica* and are perhaps the oldest of garden roses, having been known for several thousand years. Their flowers, often 7.5cm (3in) wide, have magnificent colours and include purple, crimson and mauve shades. They appear during early and mid-summer, on stiff stems. Varieties to consider include:
• 'Belle de Crécy': (*below left*).
• 'Belle Isis': Richly fragrant, rich cerise-pink becoming soft

parma-violet; 90cm/3ft high and wide.
• 'Empress Josephine': Excellent shrub. Clear rose-pink flowers with deep-pink veins; 90cm (3ft) high and wide.
• 'Officinalis': Often known as the Apothecary's rose, it has large, light-crimson flowers with golden stamens; 1.2m (4ft) high and wide.
• 'Rosa Mundi': A sport from 'Officinalis', with crimson flowers striped with white; 1.2m (4ft) high and wide.
• 'Tuscany Superb': Fragrant, with dark maroon-crimson flowers; 1.5m (5ft) high and 90cm (3ft) wide.

'Madame Hardy' is a magnificent Damask rose. It was introduced in 1832 and is well-known for its beautiful, pure white flowers. When the blooms first open they are cup-shaped. Later they become flat. This is a good rose for a border.

'Belle de Crécy' is a Gallica rose, introduced in 1848 and still widely acclaimed by rose experts for its richly fragrant, cerise-pink flowers which slowly become a soft parma-violet. Bushes are 1.2m (4ft) high and 90cm (3ft) wide, nearly thornless and with strong, arching growth.

LEFT 'Buff Beauty' is a widely acclaimed Hybrid Musk, introduced in 1939 and revealing arching, sturdy growth and dark-green leaves, bronze when young. The Tea rose-scented, warm, apricot-yellow flowers are borne in large trusses on plants 1.5–1.8m (5–6ft) high and wide. In the latter part of early summer it is superb when planted with companions such as *Nepeta × faassenii*, *Papaver orientale* 'Perry's White', and light-orange bearded irises in a wide frill around it.

HYBRID MUSK ROSES

These are derived from *R. moschata* (Autumn Musk rose) and therefore have scented flowers during late summer and until the first frosts of autumn. Some of the best varieties include:
* 'Ballerina': Slightly scented, blossom-pink flowers; 1.2m (4ft) high and wide.
* 'Buff Beauty': (*see above*).
* 'Felicia': Strongly fragrant, silvery-pink flowers which resemble those of Hybrid Teas; 1.5m (5ft) high and wide.
* 'Penelope': (*see below*).
* 'Prosperity': Scented, ivory-white flowers borne in large trusses; 1.8m (6ft) high and 1.2m (4ft) wide.

HYBRID PERPETUAL ROSES

These were very popular in Victorian and Edwardian times, and the progeny of China, Bourbon and Portland roses. They develop large, cabbage-like flowers from early summer to the frosts of autumn. Varieties include:
* 'Baron Girod de l'Ain': Dark crimson, with a thin white band; 1.5m (5ft) high and 1.2m (4ft) wide.
* 'Ferdinand Pichard': (*see above right*).

* 'Gloire de Ducher': Fragrant, deep crimson, turning purple; 1.8m (6ft) high and 1.2m (4ft) wide.
* *'Reine des Violettes':* Shades of lilac and purple; 1.2m (4ft) high and 60cm (2ft) wide.

HYBRID SWEETBRIARS

These are also known as Penzance Briars and are richly scented, with saucer-shaped flowers during mid-summer. Crimson-scarlet hips appear in autumn. Varieties include:
* 'Amy Robsart': Rich, rose-pink; 2.4m (8ft) high and wide.

* 'Janet's Pride': Bears bright, cherry-pink flowers with nearly white centres; 1.8m (6ft) high and 1.5m (5ft) wide.
* 'La Belle Distinguée': Known as the double scarlet sweetbriar, it develops cherry-red flowers; 1.2 m (4ft) high and 90 cm (3ft) wide.
* 'Lady Penzance': Coppery salmon-pink; 1.8m (6ft) high and wide.

'Ferdinand Pichard', a Hybrid Perpetual rose raised in California and introduced in 1921, develops richly fragrant, globular, pink flowers striped crimson and purple. These are produced throughout summer and into autumn. Bushes grow about 1.2m (4ft) high and 90cm (3ft) wide. Its perpetual-flowering nature makes it a superb rose for inclusion in all gardens.

LEFT 'Penelope', a Hybrid Musk and introduced in 1924, forms a strong, branching shrub about 1.8m (6ft) high and wide. Its fragrant, creamy-pink flowers are borne in large trusses. These are followed by coral-pink hips.

MOSS ROSES

These are sports (natural mutations) of *R. centifolia* 'Muscosa' or hybrids derived from it. Moss roses develop flowers up to 7.5cm (3in) wide during the latter part of early summer and into mid-summer. They are distinguished by having stems, branches and leaf-stalks covered in bristles, and with the outer parts of flowers smothered in resin-scented mossy glands. These are less discernible in the hybrids. Varieties include:
• 'Comtesse de Murinais': Blush-pink, opening flat and fading to white; 1.8m (6ft) high and 1.2m (4ft) wide.
• 'Général Kléber': Soft mauve-pink and quartered; 1.2m (4ft) high and wide.
• 'Gloire des Mousseux': Fragrant, clear pink, fading with age; 1.5m (5ft) high and 90cm (3ft) wide.
• 'Louis Gimard': (*see below*).
• 'Maréchal Davoust': Fragrant, intense carmine-pink, later lilac; 1.2m (4ft) high and wide.

• 'Old Pink Moss': Also known as Common Moss and *Centifolia muscosa*. Fragrant and clear pink; 1.2m (4ft) high and wide.

PORTLAND ROSES

These are hardy and compact bushes, often suckering and producing Damask-type flowers up to 7.5cm (3in) wide, mainly during the latter part of early summer and in mid-summer but frequently continuing to late summer and autumn. The flowers are borne singly or in small clusters. Varieties include:
• 'Comte de Chambord': warm-pink and heaviliy-fragrant (*see right*).
• 'Delambre': Deep pink and full-petalled; 90cm (3ft) high and 75cm(2^1/$_2$ft) wide.
• 'Marbrée': Deep purple-pink and opening flat; 1.2m (4ft) high and 90cm (3ft) wide.
• 'Rose de Rescht': Purple crimson and very fragrant; 90cm (3ft) high and 75cm (2^1/$_2$ ft) wide. (*see below right*).

'Comte de Chambord', a Portland rose introduced in 1860, forms an erect shrub about 1.2m (4ft) high and 90cm (3ft) wide. The heavily fragrant, warm-pink flowers with lilac tones become flat and quartered. It is an excellent shrub for a small garden, repaying the space it needs with the creation of superb fragrance and beautiful flowers.

'Louis Gimard', a Moss rose and introduced in 1877, bears hard, densely packed buds which open to reveal fragrant, large, globular, cupped flowers. They are rich lilac-cerise, flushed and veined in lilac. It forms a bush about 1.5m (5ft) high and 90cm (3ft) wide. Like all Moss roses, it inspires nostalgia for the late Victorian era when they were widely grown.

BELOW 'Rose de Rescht', usually classified as a Portland rose but by other authorities as a Damask, forms a bushy shrub with very fragrant, purple-crimson flowers. It grows about 90cm (3ft) high and 75cm (1^1/$_2$ ft) wide.

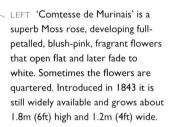

LEFT 'Comtesse de Murinais' is a superb Moss rose, developing full-petalled, blush-pink, fragrant flowers that open flat and later fade to white. Sometimes the flowers are quartered. Introduced in 1843 it is still widely available and grows about 1.8m (6ft) high and 1.2m (4ft) wide.

'Lady Hillingdon' is a remarkable Tea rose. It was raised in 1910, has richly coloured flowers and a strong tea scent. It is much hardier than most Tea roses. There is also a climbing form of this superb rose.

SCOTCH ROSES

These owe their parentage to the Scotch rose or Scottish rose (*R. spinosissima*), also known as the Burnet rose (sometimes spelt Burnett). They are vigorous and suckering and often spread rapidly. As their botanical name indicates, they are spiny or bristly. This group derives one of its common names from its leaves which resemble those of the English herb salad burnet, and is called the Scotch rose after nurserymen in Scotland who developed and raised new varieties. These roses have fragrant, saucer-shaped flowers up to 36mm ($1^1/_2$ in) wide, singly or in small clusters, during early and mid-summer. Varieties to consider include:
- 'Andrewsii': Clear-pink flowers with yellow stamens; 90cm (3ft) high and wide.
- 'Double White': Sweetly fragrant (said to resemble lily-of-the-valley), fully-double, globular, white flowers; 1.5m (5ft) high and 1.2m (4ft) high.
- 'Dunwich Rose': Pale-lemon flowers amid fern-like leaves; 60cm (2ft) high and 90cm (3ft) wide.
- 'Falkland': Semi-double and pink, fading to near white; 1.2m (4ft) high and wide.
- 'Mary Queen of Scots': Small, double purple and lilac flowers; 90cm (3ft) high and wide.
- 'Stanwell Perpetual': Sweetly scented, pale blush-pink flowers that open flat; 1.5m (5ft) high and wide. An excellent rose.
- 'William III': Semi-double, purplish-crimson flowers fading to lilac-pink, followed by small maroon hips; 60cm (2ft) high and wide.

TEA ROSES

These are not usually put with Old roses, but they are mentioned here because many of them have a long history and they are superb shrubs which make a notable contribution to the varied rose kingdom.

In 1824, a sulphur-yellow rose was introduced from China and became known as a Tea rose because its fragrance was thought to resemble the bouquet of tea imported from Bengal in the same ships. The roses therefore were called Tea roses and, sometimes, Bengal roses. Varieties include:
- 'Dr Grill': Rose-pink.
- 'Lady Hillingdon': (*see right*).
- 'Mme Bravy': Fragrant, creamy-white, shaded buff.
- 'Marie van Houtte': Fragrant, cream tinged carmine-pink.

MODERN SHRUB ROSES

This is an all-embracing group of shrub-type roses, developed in the twentieth century from a wide range of parents but mostly modern bush roses such as Hybrid Teas and Floribundas, as well as Species roses and strong Ramblers. There are many other roses in the genetic cauldron of some varieties.

Most Modern Shrub roses flower intermittently throughout summer, developing flowers either singly or in small clusters. These shrubs have a robust nature and create spectacular displays in garden borders. Some are large, perhaps 2.7m (9ft) high; others are less than half this size and are more easily accommodated in gardens.

Some varieties of Modern Shrub roses have a low and, perhaps, sprawling nature, making them ideal for smothering ground with colour. These varieties are featured on pages 77. Additionally, there are shrub-type roses which are usually classified in catalogues as English roses. Some of these are discussed on pages 106 and 107. In some catalogues, both Modern Shrub roses and English roses are listed as 'modern hybrids'.

The wealth of varieties within the Modern Shrub roses is wide and there are many others in addition to the ones featured here. These include:
* 'Aloha': As well as creating a shrub about 1.5m (5ft) high and wide, it creates a superb pillar rose and is shown on page 91. It develops fragrant, clear-pink flowers.
* 'Armada': Hybrid Tea-like, soft rose-pink flowers born on branching stems; 1.2–1.5m (4–5ft) high and wide.

* 'Autumn Fire': Deep blood-red flowers and orange-red hips; about 1.8m (6ft) high and wide.
* 'Bloomfield Abundance': Blush-pink; 1.8m (6ft) high and 1.5m (5ft) wide.
* 'Erfurt': Semi-double, fragrant, clear-pink flowers that deepen towards their edges; 1.5m (5ft) high and 1.2m (4ft) wide.
* 'Fountain': Hybrid Tea-like, rich, velvety, blood-red flowers borne in clusters on upright

shrubs; 1.8m (6ft) high and 1.5m (5ft) wide.
* 'Fred Loads': Sometimes this is classified as a large and vigorous Floribunda. It bears semi-double, orange-vermilion, fragrant flowers amid masses of leaves; 1.8m (6ft) high and 1.2–1.5m (4–5ft) wide.

'Fritz Nobis' forms a 1.8m (6ft) high and wide shrub drenched in clove-scented, fresh-pink flowers with darker shading during early summer. The flowers are enhanced by a few yellow stamens. Later, there is a crop of round, dull-red hips. It was introduced in 1940.

RIGHT 'Cerise Bouquet', introduced in 1958, has a graceful and arching habit, with semi-double, raspberry-scented, cerise-pink flowers in open spray in early summer. It does not repeat its flowering, but nevertheless is well worth growing. It forms an imposing shrub, 2.7m (9ft) high and 2.4–3.6m (8–12ft) wide, with small, greyish leaves. This beautiful shrub results from a cross between R. multibracteata and 'Crimson Shower', a Rambler.

• 'Frühlingsanfang': Sweetly fragrant, ivory-white flowers and maroon-red hips; 2.7m (9ft) high and wide.

• 'Frühlingsgold': Heavily fragrant, pale-yellow with deep-yellow stamens; 2.1m (7ft) high and wide.

• 'Golden Wings': Yellow flowers with mahogany-coloured stamens; 1.2m (4ft) high and wide.

• 'Jacqueline Dupré': It is related to Scotch roses and bears dainty, blush-white, semi-double flowers about 10cm (4in) wide. The flowers have a musk-like fragrance and bushes grow about 1.8m (6ft) high and 1.2–1.5m (4–5ft) wide.

• 'James Mason': This is a cross between 'Tuscany Superb' and 'Scarlet Fire'. It develops semi-double, rich-crimson, fragrant flowers during early summer and amid attractive leaves; 1.5m (5ft) high and 1.2m (4ft) wide.

• 'Lavender Lassie': Fragrant, double flowers, pink shaded with lavender, in large clusters: 1.2m (4ft) high and 90cm (3ft) wide.

• 'Magenta': The richly scented, rosy-magenta to pale-mauve flowers have an old-fashioned appearance; 1.5m (5ft) high and 1.2m (4ft) wide.

• 'Marchenland': Introduced in 1951, it has a very vigorous Hybrid Tea rose in its parentage, as well as a slender connection with Hybrid Musks. It develops fragrant, semi-double, open, clear-pink flowers; 1.2m (4ft) high and 90cm (3ft) wide.

• 'Marguerite Hilling': This is a superb pink-flowered sport of the well-known 'Nevada' (*see right*).

It forms a round shrub, about 2.1m (7ft) high and wide.

• 'Marjorie Fair': Deep-red with a yellow eye; 1.2–1.5m (4–5ft) high and wide.

• 'München': Strongly garnet-red with a few white streaks; 1.5m (5ft) high and wide.

• 'Nymphenburg': Sweetly apple-scented, double, warm salmon-pink flowers shaded cerise-pink and orange, with a yellow base to the petals; 2.4m (8ft) high and 1.8m (6ft) wide. It also develops large, turban-like orange-red hips.

• 'Pearl Drift': The almost double flowers are mainly white but with a pink flush. They are borne on compact but sprawling bushes that grow to be about 90cm (3ft) high and 1.2m (4ft) wide.

• 'Sally Holmes': Creamy-white flowers borne on strong, vigorous shrubs; 1.2m (4ft) high and wide. Each bush appears to be almost continually in flower.

• 'Scarlet Fire': Brilliant-scarlet, single flowers with golden stamens borne on arching stems. After the flowers fade the bush develops large, red hips (fruits). Bushes grow about 2.1m (7ft) high and wide.

LEFT 'Frühlingsmorgen', introduced in 1941 and with a form of the Burnet or Scotch rose (*R. spinosissima*) in its parentage, is highly acclaimed for its robust nature and spectacular, rose-pink flowers with yellow centres and purplish-maroon stamens during early summer. Sometimes it repeat-flowers, with a small crop in late summer. Bushes grow about 1.8m (6ft) high and 1.5m (5ft) wide. The foliage is leaden-green. After flowering, it develops large, maroon-red hips.

'Scarlet Fire', introduced in 1952, becomes drenched in single, bright-scarlet flowers with golden stamens during early and mid-summer. These are followed in late summer and autumn by long-lasting, pear-shaped red hips. Bushes grow about 2.1m (7ft) high and 2.1–2.9m (7–9ft) wide.

'Nevada', a dominant shrub introduced in 1927, creates a mass of 10cm (4in) wide, semi-double, creamy-white flowers with a blush tint early in the rose season, followed intermittently by further ones. Bushes grow about 2.1m (7ft) high and wide.

ENGLISH ROSES

English roses encompass an increasingly popular and widely grown group of shrub-style roses. They have been bred during relatively recent years by David Austin Roses of England and have a recurrent flowering nature. Their colour range is wide, with soft colours, superb fragrance and the distinctive charm of Old roses.

These roses result from the hybridizing of modern varieties with Old roses. The range of varieties is wide and each year further ones are added. Many are small enough to fit into the smallest garden; 'Pretty Jessica', for example, is only 75cm (2¹/₂ ft) high. Others are 1.5m (5ft) high, while some such as the well-known and widely grown 'Gertrude Jekyll' can be encouraged to climb as well as to form a superb shrub.

LOOKING AFTER ENGLISH ROSES

They require similar attention to that given to other roses, but because they are expected to flower over a long period they must be fed and watered regularly, especially during mid-season. Additionally, prepare the soil well by adding well-decomposed manure before planting them.

The range of varieties is wide and many are illustrated and featured on these pages. They include:
* 'Abraham Darby': Rich, fruit-like fragrance and deeply cupped flowers in shades of apricot and yellow; 1.5m (5ft) high and wide (*see right*).
* 'Chianti': Old-rose fragrance, with deep-crimson flowers which become purplish-maroon with age; 1.5m (5ft) high and wide. It flowers only once in the rose season.
* 'Constance Spry': Old-fashioned type, clear-pink flowers with a myrrh-like fragrance; 1.8–2.1m (6–7ft) high and wide. It flowers only once in the rose season, and can also be grown as a climber, up to about 3.6m (12ft) high.
* 'Dapple Dawn': Large, single pink flowers appear almost continuously throughout the rose season; 1.5m (5ft) high and 1.2m (4ft) wide.
* 'Fair Bianca': Pure white flowers, becoming saucer-shaped; 90cm (3 ft) wide.
* 'Gertrude Jekyll': Heavily scented, and rich rose-pink; 1.2m (4ft) high and about 1m (3¹/₂ ft) wide.
* 'Graham Thomas': Refreshing Tea rose fragrance and golden-yellow flowers; 1.2m (4ft) high and wide.
* 'Heritage': Lemon-like fragrance, with soft-pink flowers; 1.2m (4ft) high and wide. It can also be grown as a low-growing Climber.
* 'Jayne Austin': Soft yellow, tending towards apricot and with an enchanting sheen; 1–1.2m (3¹/₂–4ft) high and about the same in width.
* 'L. D. Braithwaite': Richly fragrant, with crimson flowers; 1m (3¹/₂ ft) high and wide.
* 'Lucetta': Fragrant, large, semi-double, soft blush-pink flowers fading to almost white; 1.2m (4ft) high and wide.
* 'Red Coat': Large, single, crimson-scarlet flowers continuously throughout the rose season; 1.5m (5ft) high and 1.2m (4ft) wide.

'Abraham Darby' develops large, deeply cupped flowers in shades of apricot and yellow. They have the bonus of a rich, fruit-like fragrance and are borne on shrubs about 1.5m (5ft) high and wide.

• 'Shropshire Lass': Delicate flesh-pink, fading to white; 2.4m (8ft) high and 1.8m (6ft) wide. It flowers only once in the rose season, and can also be grown as a climber up to 3m (10ft) high.

• 'The Countryman': An Old-rose fragrance and clear-pink flowers, with a touch of Portland rose in its genes; 90cm (3ft) high and usually about 1m (3½ft) wide.

• 'Winchester Cathedral': White flowers at intervals throughout summer; 1.2m (4ft) high and wide.

ABOVE 'Gertrude Jekyll', named in honour of the legendary English garden designer who died in 1932, develops strongly fragrant, rosette-shaped, rich-pink flowers on shrubs about 1.2m (4ft) high and 1m (3½ft) wide.

'Red Coat' is famed for its ability to create a floriferous display of large, single, crimson-scarlet flowers throughout the rose season. These are borne on shrubs 1.5m (5ft) high and 1.2m (4ft) wide.

'Shropshire Lass', a cross between 'Mme Butterfly' and 'Mme Legras de St. Germain', forms a superb shrub about 2.4m (8ft) high and 1.8m (6ft) wide. The large, flat, flesh-pink flowers slowly fade to white. It can also be grown as a Climber, when it grows about 3m (10ft) high.

'Graham Thomas', named after one of the most influential gardeners and rose authorities of the twentieth century, develops pure-yellow flowers with a strong Tea rose fragrance. It forms a shrub about 1.2m (4ft) high and wide.

GLOSSARY

acid soil Soil which has a pH of less than 6.5.

American Rose Society A North American rose society, founded in 1899.

anther Part of the male reproduction system where pollen is housed. An anther is supported by a filament and they are collectively known as stamen.

axil Correctly, the angle between a leaf-stalk and the shoot which bears it. More usually, the junction of a leaf or shoot with a stem.

balling A physiological disorder, when the outside petals of a flower cling together (see page 20).

bare-rooted Young rose plants are often sold with bare roots. This means that they have been dug up during their dormant period so that they can be sent to a customer (see page 13).

bleeding The loss of sap from a stem as a result of being pruned too late in spring – after the sap has started to rise.

blind shoot A physiological disorder when a shoot fails to develop a flower.

bloom Used as an alternative term for a flower. Can also be used to mean a waxy, powder coating.

blown When a flower is fully open and the petals are starting to fade or fall off.

boss A ring of stamens, forming a decorative and prominent feature.

bract A botanical term for a modified leaf which develops in the axils of leaves or on flower stems. In roses it is green, but in other plants may be brightly coloured.

breaking bud A bud as it starts to open.

bud A flower before it opens. Inside a bud, the petals and other flower parts are tightly folded and covered by closely overlapping, scale-like growths collectively known as the calyx.

budding The unifying of a bud (variety part) with a rootstock.

bud union The position where a plant is budded.

button eye Occurs at the centres of the flowers on some Old roses. Some of the petals fold inwards to form a button.

callus Hard tissue which forms over a pruning cut or other damaged surface.

calyx Green, somewhat scale-like tissue which protects the flower when at its bud stage.

compost It has two meanings. One is vegetable material placed in a heap and encouraged to decompose so that eventually it can be dug into soil or used to form a mulch. The other meaning is a compost (mixture of sharp sand, moist peat and sterilized soil) in which seeds are sown, cuttings rooted and plants grown. Some composts are peat-based.

cross The resultant progeny from cross-pollination.

cultivar A variety raised in cultivation. Properly, the vast majority of modern varieties should be known as cultivars, but as the term 'variety' is by far better known this has been used throughout this book.

cutting A healthy piece of a plant, detached and encouraged to develop roots.

dead-heading The removal of faded or dead flowers to encourage the development of further ones.

de-shooting The removal of shoots to ensure that the remaining ones have more light and air.

die back When a shoot decays backwards from its tip.

disbudding The removal of small buds from around a main flower to encourage its development.

dormant period When a plant is not actively growing. For a rose in a temperate region, this would be from late autumn or early winter to late winter or early spring.

double-flowered Refers to the number of petals present. Some double flowers are said to be 'moderately full' (21 to 29 petals), others 'full' (30 to 39 petals), while some are 'very full' (40 or more).

fertilization The fusion of a male gamete with ovules (female part of a flower).

filament The small, usually narrow, stalk which supports an anther.

Floribunda roses These are now properly known as Cluster-flowered roses. However, they are usually listed in catalogues by their earlier name, which is also better known to gardeners. Throughout this book, therefore, the earlier name has been used.

floriferous Term to indicate an abundance of flowers.

flush A period when flowers are opening. Some varieties have repeated flushes.

foliar feeding Spraying foliage with fertilizers as a way to apply nutrients.

fungicide A chemical used to prevent or control a disease.

genus A botanical classification of related plants. Within a genus there could be one or more species.

grandiflora A North American term for large Floribundas that have Hybrid Tea-like flowers.

heeling-in The temporary planting of bare-rooted plants in winter, while waiting for the weather to improve so that they can be re-planted in their more permanent positions.

hep The fruit of a rose (see page 6). Also known as a hip.

hip An alternative term for hep.

hybrid An offspring from two parents of different species.

Hybrid Tea These roses are now properly known as Large-Flowered roses. They are usually listed in catalogues by their earlier name, by which they are better known to gardeners, therefore, throughout this book the earlier name has been used.

inflorescence The arrangement of flowers on a stem.

insecticide A chemical used to kill insects.

maiden A plant in its first year after being budded.

mulch The formation of a layer of organic material around plants – but not touching their stems.

mutation The spontaneous change in part of a plant. This includes greater or lesser vigour, larger or smaller flowers, and a change in colour. This often leads to the development of new varieties. Also known as sports.

neutral Refers to soil which is neither acid nor alkaline, having a pH of about 7.0.

node The position on a stem where a leaf or bud arises.

once-flowering A single flush of flowers, generally lasting for several weeks. Some varieties with this nature also produce a few flowers in autumn, but not sufficiently to be called a second flush.

pedicel A flower stalk.

pH A scale from 0 to 14 that defines the alkalinity or acidity of soil. A pH of 7.0 is neutral: figures above it indicate increasing alkalinity, while below greater acidity

pollen Dust-like material containing male characteristics. It is produced in the anthers of plants.

pollination The transference of pollen from anthers (male part of a flower) to the stigmas (female part). Fertilization does not necessarily follow pollination.

propagation The creating of further plants. In the case of roses, this is usually by budding, although some can be layered, while cuttings

taken of others. Some can be raised from seeds.

quartered Refers to the arrangement of petals in a flower, when the flower appears to be formed of four distinctive parts.

recurrent The production of two or more flushes of flowers during the same flowering season.

remontant An alternative term for recurrent.

repeat-flowering This means the same as recurrent.

reverse With roses, it is used to refer to the side of a petal which is away from the flower's centre.

reversion Usually used to refer to a mutation (sport) which reverts to the nature of the parent. May also refer to plants which have been neglected and overwhelmed with suckers arising from the roots.

rootstock The root part on to which a bud is inserted (see page 18).

Rosa The genus in which all roses belong.

Rosaceae Refers to the family of flowering plants, typically having five-petalled flowers.

scion The term for the bud which is budded on to the rootstock.

semi-double flowers Refers to the number of petals present (from 8 to 20).

single flowers Refers to the number of petals present (less than 8).

species A classification of related plants within a genus. Within the rose genus there are said to be more than 3,000 names of specific rank. No more than 150 of these are garden-worthy plants.

sport Another term for mutation.

stamen The male part of a flower, formed of an anther and filament.

stigma The female part of a flower upon which pollen alights.

stipule A leaf-like growth at the base of a leaf-stalk.

style Female part of a flower. It connects the stigma with the ovary.

sucker Growth which arises from the rootstock of bush roses, or stems of standard types. They must be removed.

systemic A pesticide or fungicide which enters a plant and travels through its sap stream.

truss A compact, terminal flower cluster.

variety At one time, all variations within a species were known as varieties. Correctly, those raised in cultivation should now be called cultivars. As the term 'variety' is much better known than cultivar (which to many people is an unfriendly term), variety has been used throughout this book.

INDEX